A
PLANTSMAN'S GUIDE TO
CLEMATIS
DR JOHN HOWELLS

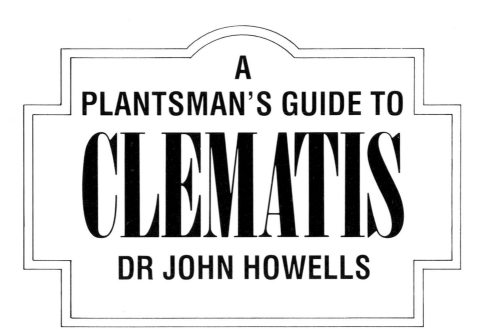

A
PLANTSMAN'S GUIDE TO
CLEMATIS
DR JOHN HOWELLS

SERIES EDITOR
ALAN TOOGOOD

WARD LOCK

AUTHOR'S ACKNOWLEDGEMENTS

The author is grateful to Jim Fisk, the doyen of British clematarians, for reading this manuscript; his suggestions gave the author assurance and added authority to the work. The author also thanks Mrs Janet Hodge for her careful preparation of the manuscript.

First published in Great Britain in 1990
by Ward Lock Limited, Villiers House,
41/47 Strand, London WC2N 5JE, England

A Cassell Imprint

Text filmset in Times Roman
by Chapterhouse Limited, Formby, England
Printed and bound in (to follow)
by Resopal

British Library Cataloguing in Publication Data

Howells, John
   A plantsman's guide to clematis.
   1. Gardens, Clematis
   I. Title
   635.933111

ISBN 0 7063 6838 X

CONTENTS

PUBLISHER'S NOTE

Readers are requested to note that in order to make the text intelligible in both hemispheres, plant flowering times, etc. are described in terms of seasons, not months. The following table provides an approximate 'translation' of seasons into months for the two hemispheres.

Northern Hemisphere		Southern Hemisphere
Mid-winter	= January	= Mid-summer
Late winter	= February	= Late summer
Early spring	= March	= Early autumn
Mid-spring	= April	= Mid-autumn
Late spring	= May	= Late autumn
Early summer	= June	= Early winter
Mid-summer	= July	= Mid-winter
Late summer	= August	= Late winter
Early autumn	= September	= Early spring
Mid-autumn	= October	= Mid-spring
Late autumn	= November	= Late spring
Early winter	= December	= Early summer

Captions for colour photographs on chapter-opening pages

pp. 8–9 'Perle d'Azur', a sky-blue gem, the world's sweeheart and the world's number one. Makes a wall of continuously flowering blooms up to 5.5 m (18 ft).

pp. 24–25 The loveliest of all rose-clematis combinations, the unique yellow single 'Mermaid' rose and the sky-blue of vigorous 'Perle d'Azur'.

pp. 58–59 The blue and white nodding bells of the early-flowering *C. macropetela* chosen to bloom with the early-flowering rhododendron and beautifully matched with its colour.

pp. 86–87 The herbaceous *C. × durandii* gives continuous summer colour to a border with blooms of indigo-blue and yellow that invites use by the flower arranger.

pp. 108–109 The viticellas will scramble freely over low-growing conifers (this one is the purple and white 'Venosa Violacea'). Given a discreet pruning, they will be unnoticeable in winter.

pp.118–119 A blaze of light from the bluish-white blooms of the vigorous *C. × jouiniana* 'Praecox' tumbling down a shrub.

EDITOR'S FOREWORD

This unique series takes a completely fresh look at the most popular garden and greenhouse plants.

Written by a team of leading specialists, yet suitable for novice and more experienced gardeners alike, the series considers modern uses of the plants, including refreshing ideas for combining them with other garden or greenhouse plants. This should appeal to the more general gardener who, unlike the specialist, does not want to devote a large part of the garden to a particular plant. Many of the planting schemes and modern uses are beautifully illustrated in colour.

The extensive A-Z lists describe in great detail hundreds of the best varieties and species available today.

For the historically minded, each book opens with a brief history of the subject up to the present day and, as appropriate,

looks at the developments by plant breeders.

The books cover all you need to know about growing and propagating. The former embraces such aspects as suitable sites and soils, planting methods, all-year-round care and how to combat pests, diseases and disorders.

Propagation includes raising plants from seeds and by vegetative means, as appropriate.

For each subject there is a society (sometimes more than one), full details of which round off each book.

The plants that make up this series are very popular and examples can be found in many gardens. However, it is hoped that these books will encourage gardeners to try some of the better, or perhaps more unusual, varieties; ensure some stunning plant associations; and result in the plants being grown well.

CHAPTER ONE

PAST AND PRESENT

Clematis is on the way back to becoming, deservedly, one of the most popular of garden plants – and the most fascinating climbing plant of all. It lost its way at the end of the last century when clematis wilt disease came on the scene. Understood at last, wilt can now be prevented by modern fungicides. Interest has been rekindled.

Close acquaintance of the clematis reveals the remarkable virtues of this climbing plant. It can produce either large plate-sized blooms or myriads of tiny flowers. It can be in bloom every month of the year. Its colour ranges from white to yellow, through pink to red, to blue to mauve. It has evergreen and deciduous forms. It can grace a rockery with a few centimetres or climb a tree to 12 m (40 ft). It has scented varieties. It even has herbaceous forms. Attractive seed heads are a special feature. It can fit into any type of garden and every corner of it. Grown properly, it is one of our hardiest plants and has a long life. It is neither a British plant, nor American, nor Australian, nor Chinese, nor Scandinavian, nor Russian – it belongs to us all.

It is not always necessary to grow a large number of clematis to derive pleasure. Even a dozen will create a diversified collection and give you the time to acquire knowledge of the characteristics of each plant. Of course, more time, space and numbers, bring added joy. But there is an optimum; too many plants call for continuous effort, leaving rarely a moment to stand and admire.

HISTORY

In the genus *Clematis* there are over 250 wild, native species (groups of individual plants with similar characteristics) – more than in roses. These grow wild in the temperate regions of the northern and, to a lesser extent, southern hemispheres, including southern Europe (for instance *C. alpina*) and the Mediterranean (*C. cirrhosa*), India (*C. montana*), China (*C. lanuginosa*), Great Britain (*C. vitalba*,

old man's beard), Japan (*C. patens*), Australia (*C. arista*), New Zealand (*C. afoliata*), and the Americas (*C. virginiana*). These native clematis are still to be found in these areas and are well recognized for their attractiveness or even medicinal use.

FIRST INTRODUCTIONS

When man began to travel he brought back to his own country plants which appealed to him. *C. viticella*, for instance, was in 1569 brought from Spain to England and renamed 'The Purple Virgin's Bower'; it is still a very popular clematis today. In 1596, three more came to England, which are also extensively grown today – *C. flammula*, *C. cirrhosa*, and *C. integrifolia*.

As time passed, botanical collections were started, and this led to a systematic search for new varieties. So, wild varieties were introduced into these collections, and even today, more wild varieties are being discovered; the search is still on. Many of the original wild species have by now been improved, either by cross breeding within the same species or by cross breeding between species. Sometimes new 'sports' appear that are more attractive than the original.

Opposite:
C. montana, *the tallest of all clematis, and true to its mountain origins soars 10 m (30 ft) and more up a tall conifer, giving a breathtaking cascade of bloom in spring. Some varieties give a bonus of fragrance.*

C. marmoraria, *the shortest of all clematis, survives in its native marble mountains to give exquisite mounds of colour; later comes a dazzling display from its large feathery seed heads.*

CROSS BREEDING

A systematic effort to improve clematis came in the 19th century and was remarkably successful. Nurseries wanted to improve their plants' appeal to the buyer. At that time, particularly fine parents for hybridizing were coming from Japan and China. These were the parents of the spectacular large-bloomed clematis, a key feature of the modern flower. These noteworthy plants were *C. florida* (abundant flowering), the large flowered *C. patens* (spreading) from Japan, the large flowered *C. lanuginosa* (downy) from China, *C. fortunei* (named after its collector, Robert Fortune) from Japan, and *C. standishii* (named after a Surrey nurseryman). All of these can still be found in their native countries; but it was the cross breeding of these plants, and the selecting of the best seedlings, that brought about plants which are a vast improvement on the original plants, and with large blooms. In the 19th century, Jackman's Nursery listed 343 clematis. Since then, of course, many more hybrids have come from deliberate or accidental crossing; today's catalogues will list up to 150 of the best.

Most of the popular large-flowered clematis today (many of them in Jackman's list) were the product of hybridizing in the last century. 'Jackmanii' which is so widely grown today, first flowered in 1862, over 120 years ago, as the result of a cross made by G. Jackman & Son in 1858. The most popular clematis of today, 'Perle d'Azur', first flowered in 1885. Other popular clematis from around that time are 'Duchess of Edinburgh', 'Elsa Späth', 'Fair Rosamond', 'Gipsy Queen', 'Henryi', 'Lasurstern', 'Lawsoniana', 'Marie Boisselot', 'Miss Bateman', 'Miss Crawshay', 'Mrs Cholmondeley', 'Proteus', 'The President', 'Victoria', 'W. E. Gladstone' and 'William Kennett'. All of these have truly stood the test of time. Eight out of ten of the most popular clematis in the International Clematis Society analysis in 1988 were available in the last century.

DISASTER AND REVIVAL

With success, however, came tragedy. At some point during all this hybridizing, a vulnerability to wilt began to appear in the new plants. (In the same way that 'black spot' came to the rose.) Such was the devastation that clematis lost their appeal, hybridizing stopped and most nurseries lost interest. It took half a century for clematis to make its way slowly back into favour, helped by a few nurseries devoted to clematis alone, careful hygiene, clear advice to the gardener, but above all the advent of the modern fungicide, more than one of which are effective in preventing wilt.

Hybridizing resumed after the Second World War with fine introductions such as 'Dr Ruppel' from Argentina, 'General Sikorski' and 'Niobe' from Poland, 'Haku Ookan', 'Myojo', 'Asao' from Japan, 'Vyvyan Pennell', 'H. F. Young', 'Mrs N. Thompson', 'Sylvia Denny' from England, 'Blue Bird' and 'Rosy O'Grady' from Canada, 'Prince Charles' and 'Snow Queen' from New Zealand and 'Serenata' from Sweden. Some time in the future, the work of the 19th-century hybridizers will come fully to fruition, and we may even have clematis immune to wilt.

THE SPECIES

At first the large-flowered cultivars (garden plants, not wild; produced by hybridization) catch the eye of the gardener. Later, looking for new interest, the species may catch his attention, for it is true to say that both cultivar and species have their worth and fascination. Some of the native species are still widely grown and are very popular, frequently in the form of new derivatives.

The clematis *C. viticella* (a vine bower) was introduced from southern Europe as far back as the 16th century and named in England 'the Purple Virgin's Bower'. At around the same time came *C. cirrhosa* (having tendrils) and *C. flammula* (a little flame) from southern Europe; also *C. integrifolia* (undivided leaves) from Hungary. *C. orientalis* (from the East) arrived in the 18th century from northern Asia, as did the hardy *C. alpina* (of the Alps) from the mountains of Europe. In the 19th century came *C. montana* (of mountains) from the Himalayas; *C. tangutica* (from the Tangut region of Tibet); also *C. chrysocoma* (golden body due to yellowish down) and *C. texensis* (of Texas) from the USA. At the start of the 20th century came the hardy *C. macropetala* (of large petals) and *C. armandii* (after the missionary, Armand David) from China.

In their own terrain, the native clematis can be a spectacular sight, for instance *C. vitalba* (a white vine) in the British Isles in late summer, or the very similar *C. virginiana* (of Virginia) in the United States. *C. arista* (pointed tips of leaves like a beard) is so prolific in one area of Victoria, Australia, that a village there is called Clematis.

CHARACTERISTICS

Clematis is a flowering plant (angiosperm). The genus *Clematis* belongs to the family of plants *Ranunculaceae* (48 genera), in common with wild plants such as buttercup and kingcup, and the garden plants anemone, delphinium, paeony and hellebore. It is classed as a woody plant as its stem becomes tough and fibrous after two or three years; even so, there are a few exceptions such as the herbaceous clematis. Clematis plants are mostly climbing, some clamber and a few are herbaceous (the stem persisting for only one season). The plants are mostly deciduous (lose leaves at the end of the growing season), but there are some evergreen exceptions. The leaves are in opposite pairs. The climbing varieties of clematis are not self clinging, but they twist for support by using a leaf stalk (petiole) as a tendril to cling with.

Clematis have one unusual feature: the petals are aborted and the sepals take on the characteristics of petals and are termed tepals. In a related genus, *Atra-*

Opposite:
Some clematis are grown for their attractive seedheads. Here are the frosted seed heads of C. tangutica *bringing beauty and interest in winter.*

gene, there is a ring of petaloid staminodes (infertile organs) between the sepals and the stamens. For convenience, atragenes are now included under the term *Clematis*. It is characteristic of clematis to have numerous stamens and they are often a striking feature of the plant. The flowers produce no nectar, only pollen. Insects are attracted by the bright tepals and stamens and visit for the pollen. The clematis plant is monoecious (has male and female flowers on the same plant) but there are exceptions; some of the New Zealand clematis are dioecious (having male and female flowers on different plants). The fruits of some clematis are so feathered as to be very conspicuous and are sometimes grown for this feature alone.

ATTRACTIONS AND FAULTS

The attractions greatly outweigh the faults. Clematis give very few problems, properly grown. They have few enemies and they are very hardy. The alpinas and the macropetalas, for instance, can stand temperatures as low as − 30°C (− 86°F). The plant has a long life, averaging a man's generation at least, and some of the montanas are said to live a century. It is a fascinating thought that most of our well known clematis have been around for well over a hundred years.

☐ THE FLOWERS

The commonest clematis colours are dark blues, purples and mauves, but this range is now being extended. We now have the clear white of, for instance, 'Marie Boisselot' (sometimes known as 'Mme Le Coultre', as Marie married); the beautiful yellow of *C. orientalis* 'Bill MacKenzie'; or the pink of 'Comtesse de Bouchaud'; the red of 'Ernest Markham' and 'Niobe'; the clear blue of 'Perle d'Azur'; the darker blue of 'Lasurstern'. The stronger the light in which the clematis is grown, the more intense the colour. If there is little light, especially early in the season, the paler clematis may show a green tinge. Too strong light, on the other hand, can lead to fading. The stamens of many clematis are very conspicuous, often coloured, and dramatically improve the impact of the flower.

Most clematis flowers are single but a number of the cultivars are double, and a few almost take on the character of a paeony. While most clematis tend to open to a flat shape, there are many variations on this. There is the tiny star of blue-white *C. flammula*, the single bell of *C. alpina*, the double bell of *C. macropetala*, the tubular bloom of *C. rehderiana*, the tulip shape of *C. texensis* and the lanterns of *C. tangutica* and *C. orientalis*.

In the species the blooms tend to be tiny but the plants make up for it by producing blooms in large numbers. The hybrids, on the other hand, can produce blooms that may be up to 25 cm (10 in) across. A well grown clematis can be very productive of blooms. There may be as many as 500 blooms on a well established plant and in the Jackmanii group this can rise to 1500. The Japanese, who specialize in growing clematis in pots, expect to get up to 200 blooms in a pot plant. Amongst the species, of course, the flowers are smaller but make up for this with a cascade of blooms. Some of the blooming can be almost continuous through the summer months.

ROUND THE YEAR CLEMATIS

It is possible to have a clematis in flower all the year round.

Mid-winter: *C. cirrhosa* var. *balearica* (*C. calycina*). **Late winter:** *C. cirrhosa*. **Early spring:** *C. armandii*. **Mid-spring:** *C. alpina*, *C. macropetala*. **Late spring:** *C. montana*, early hybrids. **Early summer:** *C. chrysocoma*, mid-term hybrids. **Mid-summer:** Jackmanii hybrids. **Late summer:** *C. viticella* hybrids. **Early autumn:** *C. flammula*. **Mid-autumn:** *C. tangutica*; *C. orientalis*, late hybrids such as 'Mme Baron Veillard', 'Lady Betty Balfour' 'Lawsoniana'. **Late autumn:** *C. maximowicziana*. **Early winter:** *C. napaulensis*.

☐ HEIGHT

Clematis vary greatly in height from the 8 cm (3 in) of *C. marmoraria*, the delightful alpine New Zealand clematis, to *C. montana* varieties which can soar 12 m (40 ft) up a tree. Tall, early species include *C. armandii*, *C. montana*, *C. chrysocoma*, *C. spooneri*. Later, in the summer, comes *C. campaniflora* and later still, in the autumn, *C. viticella* varieties, *C. flammula* and *C. rehderiana*. The tall-growing species are particularly valuable for covering an unsightly feature in the garden or climbing a tree. The tall-growing large bloomers are good for peeping in at a first floor window, or for reaching round a corner, or for stretching over a wall. The short-growing cultivars can be equally useful. They can be grown with the tall-growing varieties and hide the bare lower stems of the latter. They are useful too in small patio areas or for growing over low walls or low shrubs.

☐ FRAGRANCE

A great joy is that so many clematis are perfumed, and some very strongly so. Sadly, this is not true of the large-bloomed clematis: amongst these only 'Fair Rosamond' can claim any strong scent, and 'Barbara Jackman', 'Duchess of Edinburgh' and 'Sylvia Denny' are faintly perfumed. The picture among the species, however, is very different: starting from *C. armandii* in the early spring, to *C. rehderiana* in the late autumn, there is a procession of sweetly scented clematis.

☐ SEED HEADS

Some clematis are grown for their eye-catching seed heads. These are bordering on the spectacular in many of the wild species. Particularly striking is *C. vitalba* in the UK. The *alpina* and *macropetala* species are the first to display their seed heads in the summer and are followed in late summer by the silky seed heads of *C. tangutica* and *C. orientalis*, to be followed still later by the silver grey of *C. flammula*.

☐ HARDINESS

Some 'clematarians' have to contend with extremely low, unfavourable, temperatures. In these conditions, there are ways to success. For instance, the local native species, which are likely to be hardy, can be grown. Again, the species *alpina* and *macropetala* are hardy to very low

The vigorous large-bloomed 'Dr Ruppel', from Argentina, displaying its eight rose-madder tepals with their carmine bars and its golden stamens. The best striped clematis.

temperatures; *C. fargesii* and *C. recta* can do well. Furthermore, the late-flowering species such as *C. viticella*, *C. × jouiniana*, *C. orientalis* and *C. tangutica* can be grown, but cut down to the ground in late autumn; if the roots are well protected they will survive the winter. The same treatment can be given to some of the late-flowering cultivars. Some of the cultivars have a good reputation in cold climates and these include 'Victoria', 'Hagley Hybrid', 'Jackmanii', 'Perle d'Azur', 'Niobe', 'Gipsy Queen', 'Comtesse de Bouchaud', and 'Ville de Lyon'. As a last resort, in extreme conditions, the clematis can even be grown in containers and brought indoors in the winter.

☐ BARE WINTERS

What are the faults of clematis? Some would complain that in winter many clematis look black and unsightly without leaves. In most cases, however, this problem can be easily overcome by pruning late-flowering species and cultivars in the autumn – a partial pruning – to be followed by a hard pruning in the spring. In those varieties requiring light pruning, the bare stalks can be hidden by planting shrubs in front of them. Some clematis are said to have bare bottoms even in the flowering period. This can be dealt with by planting a short-stemmed clematis alongside the long-stemmed clematis. Or again, it is possible to bring down some of the high flowering trusses nearer the ground. The very vigorous montanas seem to be the most notable sufferers of bare stems in winter. Thus, these should be planted where they are not seen from the house during this period.

Then, in the late spring, one can walk to a vantage point to enjoy their spectacular blooming.

Another complaint is the tendency of some of the more vigorous clematis to tangle with one another, thus making a thick wad of bloom. This is really the result of defective pruning which, if correctly done and with proper training, will spread the clematis plant out so that the flowers can be seen to advantage.

CLASSIFICATION

At one time it was usual to distinguish the genus *Clematis* from related genera, such as the genus *Atragene* (which includes the alpinas and macropetalas), the genus *Viorna* (which includes American varieties such as *texensis*), and the genus *Clematopsis* (opsis, like; like a clematis) found in South Africa. Now it is usual to include all of these under the one term *Clematis*.

Until recently, clematis were typed according to the prominent parent in their breeding, for example the *patens* type, the *lanuginosa* type, the *florida* type, etc. However, as there has always been so much cross breeding, this typology has become worthless.

Today a useful and practical classification is employed. Clematis are divided into two groups according to the flowering time during the year, be it either early (Group I) or late (Group II). This latter also gives a clue to pruning (see Chapter Four): in general, the early-flowering clematis will require little pruning and the late-flowering clematis require much pruning. Each group is also subdivided into (*a*) the small-flowered species, and (*b*) the large-flowered cultivars.

The large-flowered cultivars have lace-like roots, have large flowers and are rarely scented. The small-flowered species, on the other hand, have fibrous, thread-like roots, have many small flowers, suffer less from wilt, are fast growers and many of them are scented.

Thus we end up with two groups of clematis. Group I: The early flowering, divided into (*a*) the early-flowering species and (*b*) the early-flowering large-flowered hybrids or cultivars. Group II: The late-flowering, divided into (*a* the late-flowering species and (*b*) the late-flowering large-flowered cultivars or hybrids; to Group II (*a*) are added the herbaceous clematis that in general need the same amount of pruning.

CLEMATIS – THE NAME

'Clematis' comes from the Greek for a vine (*klema*). Using the botanical name for the plant, it would be correct in pronunciation to use a long 'e' as in the original Greek, *kleema*, and therefore we could correctly use *Kleematis*, for example *Kleematis alpina*.

But the correct anglicized name in common usage is *Klematis* with a short 'e' (as in clement), then a separate 'a' (as in amoeba, or Africa), and finally 'tis' (as in hiss). So we emphasize the first fraction 'clem', break after the 'm', then comes 'a', and we end in 'tis' – 'clem-a-tis' which sounds like klaymatis (not kleematis). Happily, the *Oxford English Dictionary*, the American *Webster's Dictionary* and

Fowler's *Modern English Usage* are agreed about the above.

The plural, clematises, is so awkward that it is never used. Thus we speak of a clematis or many clematis. From the best advice I can get, it appears that the proper term for a clematis enthusiast is a 'clematarian', and for a clematis garden is a 'clematarium'.

STRUCTURE

This can be seen in Fig. 1, along with the descriptive list:

☐ LEAF
Leaflet – part of a leaf
Petiole – attaches leaf to stem
Petiolule – attaches leaflet to petiole
Bracts – modified leaves growing near flower

☐ FLOWER
Tepals – the petals of clematis
Flower bud
Peduncle – a stalk bearing flower cluster
Pedicel – a stalk bearing one flower

☐ STAMEN (male reproductive part)
Filament – stalk of stamen
Anther – contains pollen
Connective – tip of anther

☐ CARPEL (female reproductive organ)
Style – stem of ovary
Stigma – receives and nurtures pollen
Ovary – produces seed
Fruit tails – showy tail to the seed.

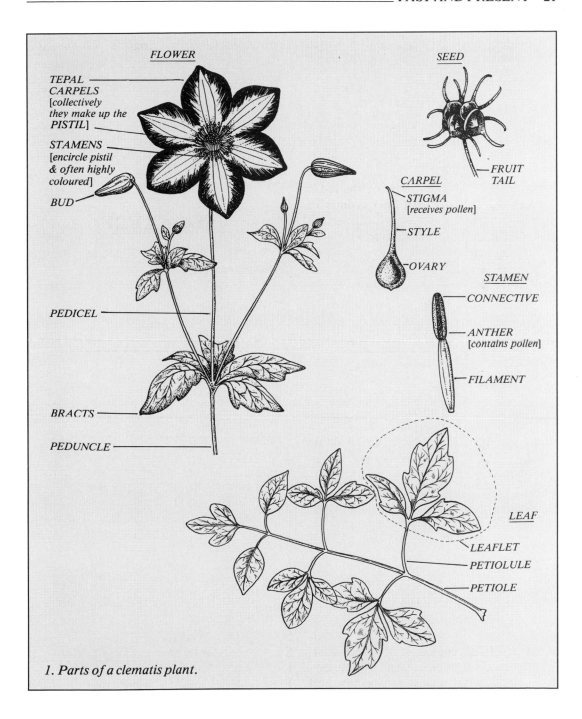

FLOWER

TEPAL
CARPELS
[*collectively
they make up the*
PISTIL]

STAMENS
[*encircle pistil
& often highly
coloured*]

BUD

PEDICEL

BRACTS

PEDUNCLE

SEED

FRUIT
TAIL

CARPEL
STIGMA
[*receives pollen*]

STYLE

OVARY

STAMEN
CONNECTIVE

ANTHER
[*contains pollen*]

FILAMENT

LEAF

LEAFLET
PETIOLULE
PETIOLE

1. Parts of a clematis plant.

MYTHS

There are two prominent ones. It is said that the clematis likes to have its feet in shade and its head in the sun. It certainly likes to have its head in the sun but the only reason for having its feet in the shade is that in the shade it is more likely to find water. Actually, to have water in the sun would be the preference of clematis. A ready way of supplying this is by mulching, to be discussed later.

It is also said that clematis prefers an alkaline soil and this notion is based on the fact that they grow strongly in chalk areas. However, it is not the alkalinity which appeals to the clematis so much as that chalk is a conspicuous reservoir of water. Again, the clematis is seeking water. Given a good supply, it will flourish happily in any soil, so long as the acidity is not extreme; in that case, like many plants, it will benefit from the acidity being reduced.

Opposite: *'General Sikorski', from Poland, shows the striking contrast of its mid-blue crenulated tepals with its golden stamens. A vigorous and outstanding newcomer.*

CHAPTER TWO

PLANTING IDEAS

There is no garden, however small, that cannot benefit from planting at least half a dozen clematis. Only in rare instances, however, are gardens completely planted with clematis – a clematarium. Clematis in the garden, as in the wild, complement and so beautify what is already there. It follows that one should look at the garden as it is and ask questions such as 'where do I need interest – or colour – or tall plants – or short plants – or fragrance?', and 'could I use a clematis?'. Or 'where are the gaps in my garden – and can they be filled by clematis?'

CHOOSING THE RIGHT NEIGHBOURS

When planting a clematis in an existing garden, it is important to bear some principles in mind. Are the flowers of the new plant meant to match the existing colours in that area or is it meant to be a contrast to them? Is the new plant meant to flower with those around it, or is it meant to flower after others have finished, and so bring colour on its own? When do I need this colour – in the spring, in the summer, the autumn or the winter? As we have seen already, there is a clematis for every season.

In general, it is best to plant the clematis of similar pruning habits as the plants around it. It also makes life easier if the clematis and its neighbours require the same growing aids – soil, fertilizers, water, light, and even fungicides. Clematis and the neighbours should have approximately the same vigour or one will kill the other in time. Adequate space must be allowed for the clematis and the plants around it; not the space required at planting but on a projection of three to four years.

Height of clematis and neighbours can be alike or can differ; if short, clematis can clothe the legs of a taller plant, or a short plant can hide the bare legs of a clematis. Clematis rarely look well in formal rows. They can look very well planted in pairs – one tall and one short, and with colours that blend, for example the blue of tall 'Perle d'Azur' with the pink of short 'Hagley Hybrid', or the mauve-red of tall 'Gipsy Queen' and the velvety red of short 'Niobe'.

CHOOSING THE RIGHT CLEMATIS

Does the situation require a blast of spectacular colour for a short time? If so, the rampant montanas, *C. chrysocoma*, *C. spooneri* and *C. × vedrariensis* are the sure answer. But this is affordable only in a large garden, when other long-flowering massed plants can follow on. A montana is not for a very small garden – it produces colour for too short a time; instead, the continuous flowering, delightful 'Mrs Cholmondeley' is a steadier friend. In a small or medium-sized garden the montanas and their like can be trimmed back after flowering to keep them in their allotted space.

The clematis must withstand the temperature you expect in the garden in the winter. A montana is not for a harsh climate; an alpina will stand it. The evergreen clematis are ideal for balmy climates but disappoint in climates with winter colds. Such, however, is the pleasure given by the evergreen *C. armandii*, with its overpowering perfume in late winter, that it is worth making an effort to find, or make, a warm sheltered corner where it will survive. Those who have conservatories or glass-covered areas, of course, can produce frost free areas and can handle the evergreens. For very low temperatures the late-flowering

Opposite:
The free-flowering bluish-purple 'Jackmanii' climbs high into a wisteria, giving it summer and autumn colour after the latter's own blooming is over.

hybrids that in any event have to be hard pruned, can receive this pruning in late autumn instead of the spring and will survive and flourish under a thick protective layer of leaves.

Some of us will feel that our gardens are full of interest and colour in the late spring and summer and it is best, therefore, to concentrate on the early- and late-flowering clematis – both species and hybrids. Not to be forgotten is the position of these early and late bloomers. They should be visible from the windows of the house, as during winter we are in the garden less often. For sheer delight in a gloomy spring, nothing can compare with the sweep of colour given by a *C. macropetala* over a low wall, up a garden post, scrambling over a shrub, or even, hopefully, placed to grow right up to the window. A little later than the macropetalas come the chrysocomas, less rampant than a montana, but strong enough to twine round and enliven that dull green conifer.

A bonus with clematis are the fluffy fruitheads which come in the autumn. They are freely produced in some of the species – *C. alpina*, *C. flammula*, *C. macropetala*, *C. orientalis*, and *C. tangutica*.

Another factor not to be forgotten is their scent. Fragrant clematis should be planted near doors and paths, where the scent is likely to be picked up by the gardener and other passers-by.

So look carefully at your garden landscape, and in particular the micro-climate (the immediate environment of a plant), and consider where you can enhance your garden by the judicious planting of these rewarding, beautiful, plants. Carefully chosen, there is a clematis for every aspect of the house, whichever way it faces.

☐ COLOUR

Having considered plant features such as hardiness, height, vigour, deciduous or evergreen, nature of leaf, scent, blooming characteristics, position and plant neighbours, the final and often deciding factor is the choice of colour. Not only must colour of tepals be considered, but also the colour of the stamens which can transform the impact of the flower. Study the contrasting dark stamens and white bloom in 'Miss Bateman', or the pure white stamens against the dark blue of 'Beauty of Worcester' and 'Lasurstern'.

The colour of the clematis must be considered, not only in relation to the plants around it, but also the background. Blue looks good against a white wall, but white against white is lost. Pink or red clematis do not blend with a brick wall. White, yellow, pink and light blue colours will light up a shady corner. A little fluorescence in a flower, as in 'Dr Ruppel' and 'Twilight', will do the same, as will a bi-coloured clematis.

Some clematis tend to lose colour in the sun, especially light colours; 'Hagley Hybrid' and 'Nelly Moser' are good examples of flowers which are inclined to fade, and are therefore better suited to light shade. A strong red like 'Niobe', or a strong purple as in 'The President', can stand full sun without fading. Thus you need to know what are the choices of reliable plants for each colour.

The bluish-purple 'Jackmanii Superba' combines with rosy-purple 'Victoria' to frame a window.

CHOICE OF COLOUR IN CLEMATIS

White – 'Duchess of Edinburgh'
'Huldine'
'Jackmanii Alba'
'Marie Boisselot'
(outstanding),
'Miss Bateman', 'Sylvia
Denny'
C. flammula
C. montana
'Grandiflora'
C. montana 'Wilsonii'
C. alpina 'Burford
White'
C. macropetala
'White Swan'

Near white – 'Henryi'
C. armandii
C. × jouiniana
C. spooneri

Yellow – 'Moonlight'
C. orientalis varieties
C. tangutica varieties

Pink – 'Comtesse de
Bouchaud'
(outstanding)
'Hagley Hybrid'
'John Warren'
'Mme Baron Veillard'
'Margaret Hunt'
'Margot Koster'
'Proteus'
C. chrysocoma varieties
C. macropetala
'Markhamii'

C. macropetala 'Rosy
O'Grady'
montana varieties
C. texensis
'Etoile Rose'

Red – 'Asao'
'Ernest Markham'
'Mme Edouard André'
'Mme Julia Correvon'
'Niobe' (outstanding)
'Rouge Cardinal'
'Ville de Lyon'
C. alpina 'Ruby'
C. texensis
'Gravetye Beauty'
C. viticella 'Abundance'
C. viticella rubra

Blue – 'Ascotiensis'
'Blue Gem'
'H. F. Young'
'Perle d'Azur'
(outstanding)
'Prince Charles'
C. alpina
'Columbine'
C. alpina
'Frances Rivis'

Deep blue – 'Beauty of Worcester'
'Elsa Späth'
'General Sikorski'
'Lasurstern'
'Mrs Cholmondeley'
C. alpina 'Pamela
Jackman'
C. × durandii
C. texensis 'Duchess of
Albany'

Red/Purple – 'Daniel Deronda'
'Gipsy Queen'
'Horn of Plenty'
'Jackmanii
   Superba'
(outstanding)
'Lady Betty Balfour'
'Lawsoniana'
'The President'
   (outstanding)
'Victoria'
'Vyvyan Pennell'

Mauve – 'Haku Ookan'
Kathleen Wheeler'
'Richard Pennell'
'W. E. Gladstone'
'William Kennett'
C. viticella
   'Purpurea Plena
Elegans'
C. viticella
   'Royal Velours'

Bi-colour – 'Barbara Jackman'
'Bees Jubilee'
'Capitaine Thuilleaux'
'Carnaby'
'Dr Ruppel'
   (outstanding)
'Lincoln Star'
'Mrs N. Thompson'
'Nelly Moser'

WALLS

These are ideal for the display of clematis. They may be the walls of a house, or a garage, or outhouses, or the high wall surrounding a garden partially or completely. Clematis can be particularly effective clambering over low walls within the garden. They are fitting, too, for the columns of an elegant portico, whether it be a colonnade or porch.

The clematis can be alone on a wall but, especially if the wall is of any length, this is not ideal as in winter the wall will be clothed in almost barren stalks. If used in this fashion, strong-growing clematis should be used such as 'Marie Boisselot', 'Lasurstern', viticellas, and the montanas. However, more effective is to allow the clematis to climb up existing climbing plants on the walls. A third way is to plant the clematis between the climbing plants.

2. Hardwood trellis.

A clematis is not self clinging and therefore needs support. Support can be given by a hardwood trellis of a 15 cm (6 in) squared mesh, fixed securely to the wall (see Fig. 2). Ideally the trellis should be the colour of the wall. Another method

Opposite:

The blue and white flowers of early-flowering, hardy, C. macropetala *herald the spring with a surge of colour as it spreads over a low wall near the house.*

is to use a galvanized wire trellis, again with 15 cm (6 in) square mesh. Also, coming on the market recently have been panels of plastic-covered steel which can be easily fixed on to walls; the panels are of various sizes (see Fig. 3). The simplest, but not the most effective method, is simply to run wire horizontally and vertically along the wall attached to nails.

Whichever method is used, they all have one requirement in common and that is they must all be away from the wall, ideally to a depth of 5 cm (2 in). This is to allow the petiole of the clematis to slip behind and attach itself to the support.

☐ PLANTING IDEAS FOR WALLS

When planting on a wall, a number of points must be borne in mind. The clematis, as will be discussed later, must be planted well away from the wall – at least 60 cm (2 ft) – and led back by string, wire or cane. The look of the clematis is greatly improved by shaping to the effect desired on the wall by judicious pruning, especially in the case of the early-flowering hybrids. The perspective is enhanced if the spread of the clematis is roughly equivalent to its height. Should the clematis prove too high for the wall, the upper tresses can be led down again towards the ground by wire or string or cane, giving a waterfall effect.

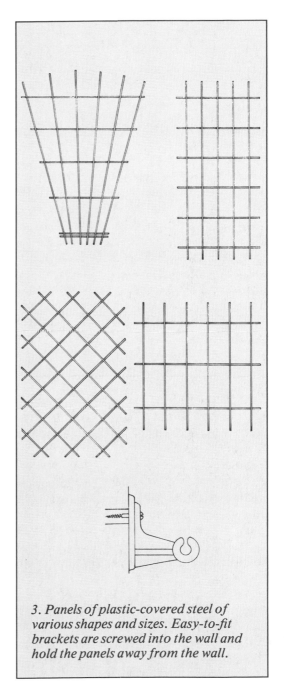

3. Panels of plastic-covered steel of various shapes and sizes. Easy-to-fit brackets are screwed into the wall and hold the panels away from the wall.

Low-growing clematis can be planted so as to hide the bare legs of a high growing clematis.

If the wall is devoted to clematis alone, a decision has to be made as to whether all the clematis are to bloom together, giving a mass effect, or whether they should follow in a sequence so as to give some interest through the year. If they are to grow with other climbing plants, they must be selected either to flower coincidentally with the host plants, or to flower when the host plants are bare of bloom. Most of the hybrid large-flowered clematis are suitable for walls either growing on their own or climbing up a host. Some of the strong-growing species, on the other hand, can kill the host plants.

Clematis are very effective clambering over low walls. This is particularly true of the macropetalas. Low-growing clematis can also give delight growing through host plants on a low wall.

Host plants may already be on the wall and thus it is simply a matter of matching the right clematis to the right host. Excellent support can be given by *Camellia japonica* varieties, ceanothus, chaenomeles, *Cotoneaster horizontalis*, *Cytisus battandieri*, escallonia, forsythia, magnolia, pyracantha and wisteria – and many others. Of all combinations the best is that of roses and clematis, but the rose will have special attention later on.

Most clematis will grow happily on south, west and east walls. However, the late-flowering large-flowered hybrids such as 'Mme Baron Veillard' and 'Lady Betty Balfour' are best on a south wall as the amount of sunshine is reduced by the time they come into bloom in the autumn.

Again, if tender evergreen clematis are to be grown they should be on a south wall.

□ NORTH WALLS

This leaves the special problem of the north wall. This may not be as big a problem as it seems, for it is surprising the number of clematis that will quite happily grow even on a shady north wall. In general vigorous clematis are suggested for a north wall, such as the alpinas, macropetalas and montanas in the spring, and vigorous growing large-bloomed hybrids during the summer. Suitable vigorous hybrids are 'Comtesse de Bouchaud', 'General Sikorski', 'Hagley Hybrid', 'Lawsoniana', 'Mrs Cholmondeley', 'The President', 'Victoria', 'Vyvyan Pennell' and 'W. E. Gladstone'. A number of hybrids are grown on north walls to bring in light – 'Miss Bateman' (white), 'Marie Boisselot' (white), 'Dr Ruppel' (rose madder), 'Perle d'Azur' (bright blue), and 'Twilight' (fluorescent mauve). One or two of the striped clematis are grown deliberately on a north wall so as to prevent fading of the bloom, for example 'Nelly Moser' and 'Bees Jubilee'. An interesting phenomenon may emerge in these north-pointing clematis. In the spring, when the intensity of light is low, the tepals may be either green or have a green tinge. To some this can be a disappointment, others find them attractive. A handful of sulphate of potash scattered round the roots in late winter will prevent this happening.

Opposite:
The climbing rose 'New Dawn' and clematis 'Perle d'Azur' contrast on a high wall at Sissinghurst.

PILLAR CLEMATIS

This term is meant to cover any artificial support given to a clematis other than by a wall. The fact is that one soon runs out of walls, and other climbing points for the clematis may have to be found within the garden itself. Furthermore, you may wish to have a display of clematis at points in the garden where there are no walls. Or you may want to give height to a display in a shrubbery or herbaceous border by introducing a clematis. Again, there may be the intention to make a special feature by introducing a post on a lawn or erecting a fence between one part of the garden and another.

A simple way of doing this is by the use of posts or poles. These should be of hardwood, and remember to bury enough of the post in the ground so that it can withstand not only the weight of the clematis but also the force of the wind. Be careful to paint your posts with a horticultural wood preservative. The clematis needs to cling to the pole and to make this possible the post should be surrounded with wire netting or by lengths of wire running vertically; the wire, of course, should be a few centimetres (1 in) away from the post so that the clematis can cling. Alternatively, it may well be that you are going to introduce a host plant on the post, in which case the clematis clings to the host.

Much ingenuity can be employed over the use of posts (see Fig. 4). It can just be a single post or it can be a row of posts along the length of a border, or along the sides of a path, or again at intervals in a shrubbery. Three posts can be brought together making a pyramid or tripod so that a number of clematis climb the pyramid. Another interesting way of employing a post is to have an umbrella at the top. The clematis climb up and then branch out on the umbrella giving the effect of a cascade of clematis. Another attractive way of display is to run a rope between two posts, or it can be a chain or wire; the clematis is encouraged to run along the support between the two posts, thus giving an effect of festooning. Moore and Jackman, in the first ever book on clematis, termed the use of a number of posts employed close together for supporting clematis as a 'climbery'. Each post will usually be able to support two clematis and a host plant; thus clematis is planted on either side of the post and led into the host plant by wires or canes. Normally, one of the two clematis on the post will be an early bloomer and the other a late bloomer. Should there be a number of posts, then of course it is possible to arrange a sequence of flowering or a mass flowering, depending upon what you prefer.

Two poles close together, joining a third pole, makes an arch. Arches can make an arbour or bower (see Fig. 4) or gazebo or rotunda. With a little ingenuity, the right mix of clematis and host, together with the natural beauty of the support, can produce a most pleasing effect.

A pergola is a natural support for clematis. It can be of simple rustic posts, hardwood, or it can be a solid structure of bricks with wooden cross pieces. It can be reserved for clematis alone, but the effect is more pleasing if there are host plants

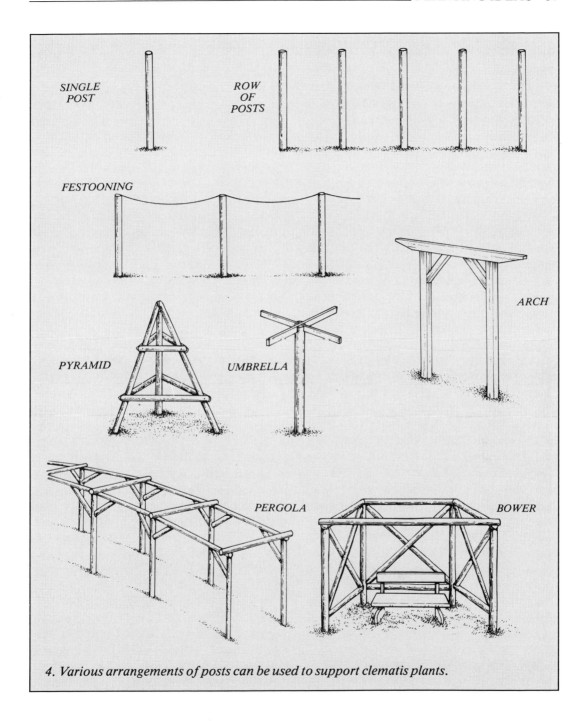

SINGLE POST

ROW OF POSTS

FESTOONING

ARCH

PYRAMID

UMBRELLA

PERGOLA

BOWER

4. *Various arrangements of posts can be used to support clematis plants.*

such as roses on to which the clematis can cling and clamber. Each post can take two clematis together with a host plant. The clematis should be matched with the host plant and there is room on a pergola to arrange a sequence of flowering through the year.

A well established garden may have natural supports within it, such as old tree stumps, large mounds, or even the roots of trees left after a great storm. Moore and Jackman referred to the latter as a 'rootery'. The idea is to allow clematis to clamber and meander at will over these natural supports, and so bring beauty to what might otherwise be an eyesore in the garden. Here vigorous clematis such as *C. montana*, *C. spooneri* and *C. × vedrariensis* come into their own. Sometimes in a garden it is not an existing natural feature that needs covering, but rather a modern construction, such as a chain link fence. This tends to be in an exposed position and will need vigorous clematis. Ideally we need clematis which need no pruning and will cover the fence throughout the year. Thus we think of the alpinas and the macropetalas. The viticellas, the tanguticas and the orientalis varieties need pruning and therefore will produce a bare fence for much of the year.

One of the most difficult areas to beautify is the roof of a shed. Wire it in horizontal lengths, and a clematis such as a *C. chrysocoma* encouraged to grow along them will give you a sensational result.

Clematis from containers can be employed to climb up posts or columns on porches, loggias, colonnades, terraces and balconies.

THE ROSE AND THE CLEMATIS

Tennyson had this to say on clematis and roses:

Rose, rose and clematis,
Trail and twine and clasp and kiss

He put on record an important truth. Clematis and roses are ideal partners; probably the best partnership in the whole garden. Unquestionably the rose is the ideal host for the clematis. This is an area yet to be exploited. They both require the same soil conditions, their climbing habits are similar, they can easily be matched for height and spread, they benefit from the same fertilizers, and the same disease control can be used for both.

They can be employed together in two ways. Firstly, when the early flowering roses have finished, clematis can be grown into the rose foliage to bring colour and interest during the rest of the year. Or, secondly, they can be grown so that the clematis enhance the flowers of the rose by complementing it. A word of warning however. Some clematis can be too strong for the strongest rose. A montana, for instance, can never be grown with a rose as it means suffocation for the rose. Again some roses can be too strong for the clematis, for example, 'Alberic Barbier' and *R. filipes* 'Kiftsgate'; the latter should be allowed to soar into a tree with a montana many yards away from it.

Some beautiful roses produce a stunning display of blooms early in the season and then, having exhausted themselves, produce few blooms later on. Examples would be 'Albertine', 'Meg',

'Maigold', and 'Zéphirine Drouhin'. After flowering, the foliage of these roses will be ready for decoration. Therefore, the whole range of the large hybrid clematis, together with the alpina and viticella varieties, can be employed. Sometimes two or three clematis can be grown into one climbing rose; it can be a judicious blend of early, middle and late-flowering clematis. Should it be desirable, for some reason, to have the rose foliage free of clematis for the winter, then it is prudent to grow the late-flowering clematis in this case, as they can be pruned early in the autumn to reveal the rose leaves again.

□ GOOD COMPANIONS

Each year the Royal National Rose Society of the United Kingdom publishes a list of recommended roses termed 'The Rose Analysis'. Taking the ten most popular climbing or rambling roses in 1989 we can speculate on desirable companions. 'Compassion' is a very strong climbing rose with pink to apricot flowers; it is said that if you can only grow one climbing rose then it should be 'Compassion'. It has a habit of tending to grow away from the wall and has to be gently coaxed back, at which it will cover a considerable space of wall. It can contend with strong-growing tall clematis, such as 'W. E. Gladstone', 'Lawsoniana' and 'William Kennett', or shorter-growing clematis such as 'Hagley Hybrid' or 'Comtesse de Bouchaud' or 'Miss Bateman'. 'Handel', of medium strong growth, has unusual cream and rose red blooms which will match any of the mauve or purple clematis. 'Golden

Showers', with its yellow flowers, is crying out for a blue clematis such as 'Perle d'Azur', 'General Sikorski' or 'Lasurstern'. 'New Dawn' is a strong grower with a multitude of light pink, beautifully shaped, and scented blooms; any strongly coloured clematis such as the reds or yellows will look good against it. 'Albertine' and 'Zéphirine Drouhin', as we have already discussed, are more suitable for being draped in clematis after flowering. This takes us to 'Schoolgirl' with its apricot-orange blooms, again a perfect match for a light or deep blue clematis. 'Pink Perpetue' is almost fluorescent; its carmine-pink blooms match any mauve, red or purple clematis – 'Jackmanii' certainly comes to mind here. The beautiful 'Maigold' has already been discussed; after a burst of bloom it is available to host any clematis. Lastly we come to 'Danse de Feu', with strong orange-scarlet blooms and a good foil for white, blue or mauve clematis. Special mention should be made of the unique, beautiful, single-flowered rose, 'Mermaid', with its large yellow blooms. Slow to grow, once it is established it can cover a very large area. Just grow it with as many plants of the clematis, 'Perle d'Azur', as it can hold. That will be a wondrous sight.

In the shrub border the shrub roses must not be forgotten and it can be rewarding to grow clematis into these. Here, there is some advantage in using the late-flowering clematis, in as much as they can be pruned back in the autumn to release the host shrub rose, or again it can be pruned at the same time as the shrub rose.

Plant the clematis at least 60 cm (2 ft)

away from the host rose. Lead the stems of the clematis into the rose with canes, string or wire. Each autumn the host rose and the clematis should be checked to ensure that neither is suffocating the other; in this event the offending plant may need to be removed or careful pruning take place so as to mitigate the damage. The roses and clematis can be fertilized together because both benefit from rich feeding. Again, the common diseases of the rose, blackspot and mildew, benefit from the same agents that prevent wilt and mildew in clematis. Thus they can regularly be treated together. Agents used against insects in the rose do not harm the clematis. Some insecticides and fungicides can be mixed and applied together.

TREES

Some general principles need to be borne in mind in growing clematis into trees. The tree should be well established before the clematis grows into it; the weight of a clematis in a strong wind is considerable and the tree must be robust enough to stand this. A chosen clematis should never be so vigorous as to suffocate the tree, nor again should a tree be so strong as to suffocate the clematis; the two must be matched. The clematis should be allowed to grow as naturally as possible in the tree; however, quite often, judicious tying-in of the clematis can help the final shape. For very tall trees it is best to employ clematis which do not require pruning. Smaller trees will probably do best with clematis that require pruning in the autumn, ie the late-flowering clematis.

This allows the tree to be tidied up for the winter and also reduces the weight on them for the winter storms. The aim is to bring interest and colour to a tree which is not blooming and which would otherwise be dull and uninteresting. Not only must account be taken of the colour of the clematis but also of the colour and form of the clematis foliage. Strong species are best for large trees. Smaller species and the large-bloomed hybrids are better for the shorter trees. In general, pale coloured or fluorescent clematis do best against dark trees and the brighter coloured clematis against the lighter trees.

☐ EVERGREENS

Evergreen trees particularly benefit from a combination with a clematis as, of course, they rarely develop spectacular flowers themselves. *C. montana*, especially its vigorous varieties, like 'Grandiflora' and 'Wilsonii', will happily clamber, with a little guidance, to 6 m (20 ft), 9 m (30 ft), 12 m (40 ft), or even 18 m (60 ft) into a large conifer. It can be a spectacular sight in the spring. A columnar conifer looks magnificent clothed in *C. chrysocoma*. Try *C. viticella* 'Etoile Violette' and 'Royal Velours' with yellow conifers. These trees frequently need to be wired to support the branches against heavy snow in the winter. The clematis can thus be tied in to the wire and guided to twine round and round the conifer foliage. Large holly trees again lend themselves to *C. montana* and *C. chrysocoma*. Smaller holly trees need a 'Huldine' or a *C. flammula*: their white bloom will show up against the dark foliage. For a variegated holly, viticella varieties would be suitable.

*A profusion of bloom from the easy-to-grow, pink and cream, 'Comtesse de Bouchaud'
match the creamy flowers of an old climbing rose.*

□ DECIDUOUS TREES

Of all the deciduous trees, none can compare with *Pyrus salicifolia* 'Pendula', whose silvery leaves are a natural foil for most of the clematis. Almost every coloured clematis will appeal against this background, except perhaps white and pale yellow clematis. *Prunus subhirtella* 'Autumnalis' is a great joy with its white or pink blossom through the winter, but for the rest of the year its leaves are somewhat insipid. The stronger viticellas could climb into it and transform it; the clematis can be pruned back for winter. Most of the prunus tend to flower briefly in the spring and can have similar treatment. This would apply also to the crataegus (hawthorns) and malus (ornamental crabs). *Robinia pseudo-acacia* 'Frisia' (false acacia) needs a foil for its glowing yellow foliage. We should consider 'Jackmanii' or 'Gipsy Queen' or *C. viticella* 'Etoile Violette'. The laburnum flowers early and thus its foliage would benefit from a clematis later; tall 'Ville de Lyon' is suitable and can be cut down in the autumn to tidy up the tree for the winter. The sorbus group tend to have fern-like foliage and a clematis can greatly enhance this; *C. viticella* 'Purpurea Plena Elegans' is a suitable choice. The acers (maples), with leaves of light hues, will benefit from viticella varieties selected to match the leaves.

□ PLANTING NEAR A TREE

It must be borne in mind that the soil and the conditions around a tree are not very kind to a clematis; the soil is often dry and has been exhausted by the tree and may

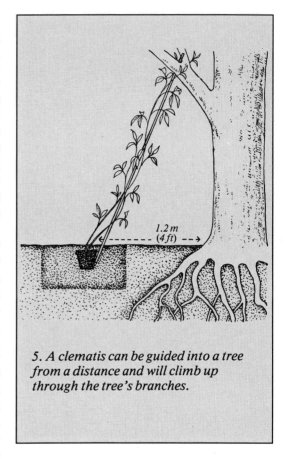

5. A clematis can be guided into a tree from a distance and will climb up through the tree's branches.

also be shaded. All these deficiencies have to be countered.

It is usual to advise that clematis should be planted on the shady side of the tree so that the light at the other side of the tree will pull the clematis through it. Furthermore, it is assumed that the clematis will benefit from any moisture in the shade. Unhappily the shade is often of such depth that the clematis refuses to take off. So it is often better to plant on the sunny side of the tree and lead the clematis into the tree by canes or string; and once it has reached the tree, it will then take its own course (see Fig. 5).

To compensate for the sun drying the ground, a heavy mulching is necessary. The clematis can be planted as far away as 1.2 m (4 ft) to 1.8 m (6 ft) from the base of the tree; in this position it is likely to have far better soil conditions than close to the tree. The rain will also reach it. Even when the clematis stems are woody and strong, a cane should always be kept alongside the stem. Then it is less easy for someone to blunder against the stem and break it; cricket on the lawn can bring awful damage.

SHRUBS

The general principles are as for trees. The shrub should be allowed to reach its optimum size and height before clematis is carried into it. It must be able to withstand the weight of the clematis. A too vigorous clematis can kill the shrub while too weak a clematis can be killed by the shrub. The shrub and the clematis must be matched for flower and foliage. The late-flowering clematis types can be pruned in the autumn and are ideal if the shrubs need to be free of clematis during the winter. Plant clematis which require the same soil and light as the host plant. Shrubs of dark foliage will match best with clematis that are light coloured; shrubs with light foliage on the other hand are more suitable with strongly coloured clematis. A shrub may be able to carry more than one clematis. Continuous flowering clematis such as 'Mrs Cholmondeley' and others are good value in that they give a long span of flowering. A long hedge can look very effective with clematis peeping over it. However, hedges need trimming, so plant late-flowering hybrids. The hedge can be trimmed in the spring and the hybrids such as 'Hagley Hybrid', 'Huldine', 'Margot Koster', 'Margaret Hunt', 'Jackmanii', 'Perle d'Azur' and others can then flower; in a long row they can look spectacular. In the autumn the clematis can be trimmed back, also allowing the hedge to be trimmed. For short shrubs the alpinas, the macropetalas and texensis varieties can be considered.

☐ SHRUB COMPANIONS

Shrubs suitable as host plants are: brooms, berberis, cornus, cotinus, cotoneaster, elaeagnus, escallonia, magnolias, shrub roses, tree paeonies and viburnums. A few suggestions will be given of suitable combinations. Ceanothus can look well after it has bloomed with the almost continuous blooming 'Mrs Cholmondeley' climbing through it – or the long-flowering cultivars 'General Sikorski' or 'Hagley Hybrid'. *Cytisus battandieri*, with its yellow flowers and silver grey foliage, is well matched by a rosy purple clematis such as 'The President'. Rhododendrons, after flowering, can be host to strong-growing early-flowering clematis such as 'Lasurstern', 'Lady Northcliffe' and 'Marie Boisselot'. *Acer palmatum* 'Atropurpureum' can be well balanced by a 'Mme Julia Correvon'. *Rosa rubrifolia* and the herbaceous clematis *C.* × *durandii* are a good team. Try blue *C. alpina* 'Frances Rivis' with white *Magnolia stellata*.

Opposite:
The lavender-blue large blooms of reliable
'Mrs Cholmondeley' beautifies an otherwise
ugly fence. The variety has a continuous
display of bloom from spring to autumn.

□ PLANTING NEAR A SHRUB

The clematis must be planted at least 60 cm (2 ft) away from the edge of the shrub and led to it on a cane, string or wire. It should be planted on the sunny side to encourage growth, and given a good mulching to retain moisture in the sun. The point of exit of the clematis from the soil must be marked with a cane, otherwise it is likely to be hoed up when you work on the shrubbery. Careful attention must be given to watering.

BORDER CLEMATIS

A number of herbaceous clematis are suitable for borders. They are a hardy group, less liable to wilt than most clematis, and of a clambering habit. They mingle with flowers and shrubs in the border in an attractive haphazard fashion, and as they have no capacity to climb or cling, they simply meander and clamber.

A particularly good variety is *C. heracleifolia* var. *davidiana* 'Wyevale', which is blue and highly scented, comes into bloom in mid-summer and continues flowering until mid-autumn. The stems are 1.2 m (4 ft) high. The flowers look and smell like a hyacinth.

Another good selection is that of *C. recta*; it has myriads of tiny, sweetly scented, white flowers, the flowers being less than 2.5 cm ($\frac{1}{2}$ in) across. The stems

are straggly and go up to 1 m (3 ft). In addition, the variety *C. recta* 'Purpurea' has handsome purple foliage when young, turning dark green later. *C. recta* comes into bloom from early to late summer. Coming into bloom in early summer also is *C. integrifolia*; this has large blue bell-shaped nodding flowers. The variety 'Rosea' is a handsome pink. *C.* × *jouiniana* has many star-shaped flowers, coloured white with a blue tinge, has no scent, can grow 3 m (10 ft) in a season, and is good as ground cover or it can mask an old tree stump. It comes into flower in early autumn, while a variety called 'Praecox' starts its season in mid-summer.

C. × *durandii* will grow up to 2 m (6$\frac{1}{2}$ ft) in a season and it happily clambers over other shrubs nearby. The flowers are abundant, of a deep indigo blue and with a distinctive eye of pale stamens. It is good as a cut flower and flowers from mid-summer to mid-autumn.

A curiosity worth growing is *C. fusca*. It has purple flowers on which there are thick woolly dark brown hairs so that the purple is hardly apparent. There are four thick tepals, which together are tulip shaped, and the pale green interior is visible. It is very hardy. The cut flowers make an arresting sight on a table.

The herbaceous types of clematis require the same rich feeding and copious watering as do the rest of the clematis. Sometimes they benefit from being grown with the support of branches over which they can clamber. Being herbaceous, the stems tend to die back in the winter. If not they should all be pruned to the ground in late winter and tidied up.

ROCKERIES

It is a surprise to many that there are clematis suitable for a rockery. The smallest known clematis comes from New Zealand and is a delightful plant suitable for a rockery. This is *C. marmoraria*, only 8 cm (3 in) high, but it can spread to 60 cm (24 in) through underground runners. The leaves are a shiny green and the solitary flowers white, flushed with green.

Three other alpine clematis come from the United States. The variety 'Tenuiloba' of *C. columbiana*, from the Rocky Mountain area, is small enough for a rockery. So is *C. addisonii* from Virginia, USA, which grows to 30–45 cm (12–15 in); the flowers are urn shaped and the colour of the sepals is rosy purple outside, with a cream within, and the anthers are also cream. Each stem, which has white heart-shaped leaves, terminates in a solitary flower. *C. albicoma* is another alpine from Virginia, 30–45 cm (12–15 in) tall.

CLEMATARIUMS

This has already been defined as a clematis garden. A number of such gardens are possible.

1. A walled garden, with a large number of clematis around the walls (see pages 31–4).
2. Climbery. This has also been discussed (see page 36) and consists of a number of poles put together to create a festooning, climbing, waterfall effect, etc.
3. A whole garden devoted to clematis. Here the aim is to use statuary, supports, shrubs and trees, simply as props on which to display a large number of different sorts of clematis. Probabaly there are as yet no gardens specifically planned in this way. It is argued that the disadvantage of such a garden is that it contradicts the natural growing fashion of the clematis, which is to clamber and climb over host plants. Thus clematis, it is argued, should be used to enhance an existing garden. However, experimentation in producing a clematis-focused garden could be of considerable interest.
4. Growing clematis on circular or oval plots. This has been tried for as long as there have been clematis. The bed can be in the region of 4 m (14 ft) in diameter. The clematis are grown in the bed and gently encouraged to cover it, either by pegging them to the ground or pegging them to supports. The bed can be given height by a statue, sundial or fountain in the middle. Some of the clematis spontaneously touching the ground can easily be layered. One variety alone can be grown or several different clematis can share a bed. There is little doubt that the more spectacular effects are produced by simply growing six or so clematis of the same variety together. Particularly suitable large-flowered hybrids are 'Perle d'Azur' (blue), 'Jackmanii' (purple), 'Comtesse de Bouchaud' (pink), 'Huldine' (white), 'Lasurstern' (blue) and 'Marie Boisselot' (white).

Some point to the usefulness of using the alpina and macropetala varieties, which although permanent and unprunable can cover 3 sq m (10 sq ft) each. The montanas can cover an even greater area, at least 6 sq m (20 sq ft). There is much to be said, however, for the

Clematis grow well in a variety of containers. Here is the early-flowering C. macropetala _'Maidwell Hall' tumbling out of a wine jar._

clematis being either the mid-summer varieties which are substantially trimmed after flowering, or the late season types which can be cut almost to the ground in the late autumn. The viticella varieties and the late-flowering hybrids, such as the 'Jackmanii' types, are particularly suitable. The advantage here is that they can be pruned back in late autumn so as to leave a tidy bed over the winter. The same argument would apply to growing the herbaceous clematis.

If the clematis are pruned back in the autumn, then the disadvantage that the beds lack foliage and colour in the late autumn and the winter can be overcome in a variety of ways. The area immediately around the bed can be planted with grey and silvery shrubs that give some interest in winter. Alternatively, here and there in the centre of the bed conifers can grow to 60–120 cm (2–4 ft). Autumn interest can be added with autumn crocus and late-flowering iris such as *Iris unguicularis*. Winter and spring interest can be added by planting with winter aconites, daffodils, tulips, hyacinths, snowdrops, crocuses, etc., together with lilies and iris. Interest can also be added by pots of geraniums in the autumn, pots of evergreens in the winter and pots of bulbs in the spring.

The clematis will require some support and this can be supplied by branches scattered over the beds or by chicken wire spread over the whole bed, or by running wire from the periphery to a central point. The clematis should be planted every 1.2 m (4 ft). Allow the clematis to grow in such a way as to cover the bare patches of the one next to it. Attention must be paid, of course, to manuring, fertilizing and copious watering.

Others believe that the clematis should clamber over a bed of plants such as cistus (rock rose), *Corokia cotoneaster*, low cytisus (brooms), hebes (shrubby veronica), lavandula (lavender), santolina (cotton lavender) and senecios. A number of such plants can be grown, or the whole bed can be devoted to one type of plant. The best effect, without a doubt, is produced by using one bedding plant and one type of clematis.

Another option, and a popular one, is to grow your clematis over a bed entirely devoted to heathers. The autumn-flowering, winter-flowering and spring-flowering heathers after blooming, are followed by mid-summer and late-flowering clematis, allowed to clamber freely over the bed. The 'Jackmanii' types, in an assortment of colours, do very well. Suitable too are the viticella varieties, the herbaceous clematis, and the texensis varieties. The orientalis varieties, well spread out, can also be effective. The cloak of clematis is pruned away in the autumn to reveal the heathers about to flower.

Similarly, a bed can be entirely devoted to low spreading conifers, with the occasional vertical conifer to give interest to the bed. Late-flowering hybrids, viticella varieties, herbaceous clematis, the texensis varieties, and the orientalis varieties can be used and, again, pruned back in the autumn. Of course, it is possible to make a bed of mixed conifers and heathers.

5. The last form of the clematarium is that of a large number of container-grown

clematis on a patio, terrace or balcony. This is very popular in countries such as Japan. A great number of different clematis of all seasons can be grown in this fashion.

CONTAINERS

Container or tub culture is for patios, terraces, roof gardens, conservatories, entrance halls, paved paths, steps and porches. It is even possible to put several 30 cm (12 in) pots in a large half-barrel and cover them with crocks or peat. Wherever there is a wall or pillar, or column, or arch which needs clothing with a clematis, but where the soil cannot reach, then a container can be used.

A pot or tub can be any size from 30 cm (12 in) upwards. The depth should be a minimum of 50 cm (18 in). The nature of the container depends on what is available, and also the use to which the container is to be put. If, for instance, a container needs a frequent move, then clearly there are advantages in it being not too heavy. On the other hand, if the container is likely to remain in one place, then it can be a large size indeed. The pot can be of any shape – square, oblong, round, and even Ali Baba style (see Fig. 6). The material can be stone, soft porcelain, earthenware, wood or plastic; the material is less important than the cultivation of the plant. One Japanese enthusiast grew a clematis, 'John Warren', in a 30 cm (12 in) pot and managed to produce 150 blooms!

Almost any type of clematis can be used in containers, depending on the aim of the planting. The early species, for instance

6. A range of containers for planting clematis

the alpinas and the macropetalas, can be very effective if blooming is wanted early in the year. Even the montanas can be grown in a large container; it can be an effective way of curbing their vigour. The early hybrids are useful in as much as they tend to be compact plants and easy to manage. The late growing hybrids and the viticellas are often the most useful of all, however, having the vigour to produce many blooms over a long time – 'Niobe' in particular has been highly praised. This type of planting also has the advantage that after an autumn pruning, the containers can be put away in a sheltered nursery bed until the following year. There is even a place for the evergreen clematis, which through using containers can be grown in a glass covered area.

□ SUPPORT

The clematis will need support and this can be given by canes which need to be from 1–1.5 m (3–5 ft) tall. The cane can be single, or there can be two or three standing vertically, or three canes can be tied at the top to make a pyramid or tripod (see Fig. 7). On the market there are a number of ingenious metal and wire supports available. Clematis benefit from growing horizontally and being gently curved around the support a number of times (see Fig. 8).

□ WATERING CONTAINERS

Special attention has to be paid to the watering of container plants and they should be checked every day. Weak, liquid fertilizer should be given every two or three days. Feeding, however, should stop when the flowers are in bloom or the blooming period will be curtailed. Clematis in containers lend themselves to foliar feeding. Naturally the plants require less water when they are dormant.

□ CHANGING THE SOIL

A clematis in its first year is usually planted in an 8 cm (3 in) pot, and in the second year should be moved to a 15 cm (6 in) pot; later still, to a 30 cm (12 in) or larger pot. In small containers the soil should be changed once a year, either in late autumn or spring; the soil below, at the sides of the plant, and above should be replaced. If necessary the clematis can be moved to a larger pot at the same time. Clematis in large containers need not have their soil changed as often. However, the top 5–8 cm (2–3 in) should be replaced with compost and bonemeal or slow-release fertilizer once a year; every few years it may be necessary to change all the soil in a large container. If the containers are outside they may need a measure of protection in the winter by a mulch of leaf-mould or bracken, and if possible moved into a sheltered part of the garden. In severely cold areas of the world the tubs may need to be taken indoors in the winter; they should not be allowed to dry out. In the garden they should be stored on shingle. Planting of a container will be discussed in Chapter 4.

UNDER GLASS

Clematis under glass can be grown in containers or in permanent beds. The first value of glass is that it allows any clematis in a pot to be forced, that is to say, flower earlier. In this way it is possible to have

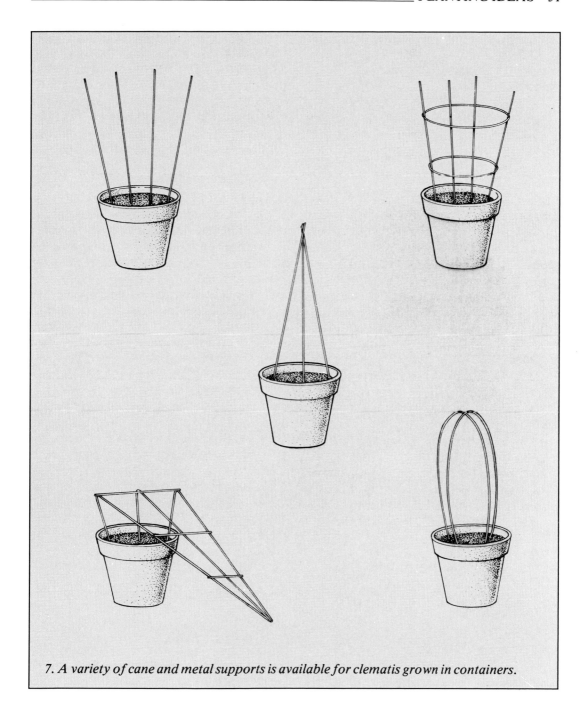

7. *A variety of cane and metal supports is available for clematis grown in containers.*

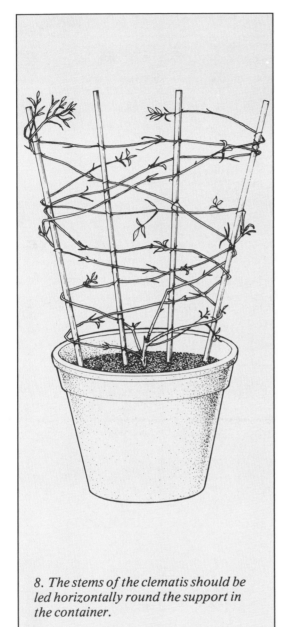

8. The stems of the clematis should be led horizontally round the support in the container.

early blooms – at least a month earlier – and therefore it is particularly useful with early-flowering hybrids. Secondly, growing under glass lends itself to growing clematis which are too tender for growing in the garden. It thus increases the range of clematis which can be grown. Thirdly, and this is probably the best use of glass, clematis can be brought into a conservatory in a sequence.

To make the third method possible there has to be a nursery bed in the garden. Here the plants are grown in pots, with flowering periods throughout the year. As each approaches the time of flowering, it is brought into the conservatory. Once the flowering is over, it returns to the nursery bed where it is nurtured for flowering the following year. While the nursery bed may be in a secluded part of the garden, it must be in full sun so that healthy, strong plants are produced. The nursery bed can have a floor of thick black polythene supported by a frame of bricks or breezeblocks. Size would depend on the number of plants to be grown. A layer of peat 23 cm (9 in) deep is put on the black polythene and the pots are placed in this. The peat should always be kept moist, and throughout the year the pots must be treated as for container-grown plants.

Almost any clematis can pass through the conservatory by the method

Opposite:
A riot of colour from a red ('Ernest Markham') and a mauve ('Lady Betty Balfour') large flowered clematis interlaced with the yellow lanterns and feathery seed heads of C. tangutica.

An autumn combination of lilac-rose 'Mme Baron Veillard' and the white 'Huldine' both climbing high into a tree.

mentioned above, but particular attention will be paid to the early tender evergreen clematis such as *C. indivisa*, *C. cirrhosa balearica* (*C. calycina*), *C. cirrhosa*, and *C. armandii*. Other tender clematis are *C. afoliata*, up to 2 m (6 ft) and with a daphne scent; *C. × vedrariensis*, up to 6 m (20 ft), which flowers in May; and *C. florida* 'Sieboldiana' which may grow up to 2.5 m (8 ft).

Also early in the season we can have the alpinas and macropetalas. Later there is a choice of spring-, summer- and autumn-flowering hybrids, the viticella varieties, orientalis varieties, as well as the texensis varieties. Late in the year, and where there is a great deal of room, it is possible to grow *C. napaulensis*, up to 5 m (30 ft).

In the conservatory, care must be taken to supply ventilation, the temperature should go no higher than 13°C (55°F) and humidity should be encouraged by syringing. Water given to clematis should be tepid, or the same temperature as the conservatory. The clematis should be regularly sprayed with insecticides and fungicides.

CUT FLOWERS

Clematis in pots do not do well in the house. But using clematis as cut flowers can be an appealing challenge for the flower arranger.

The flowers to be cut must be carefully selected; discard any damaged flowers, spent flowers or flowers on a weak stem. Cut in the evening. The flower should not be quite fully open and should be on a strong stem. Having cut the clematis stem, the leaves are then removed so as to prevent loss of water by transpiration from the leaves. The ends of the stems are crushed and dipped in boiling water for a few seconds. They are then immersed in water up to their necks and left overnight. It is said that the flowers benefit from a little sugar in the water, a pinch of fertilizer, and some would say a drop of gin!

In the spring, material will be available from the alpinas and macropetalas, and the early hybrids such as 'Dr Ruppel', 'Bees Jubilee', 'Nelly Moser' and 'Lasurstern'. Even earlier in the spring, there is double pleasure to be obtained from the blooms of *C. cirrhosa* or *C. cirrhosa balearica* (*C. calycina*) and the lovely *C. armandii*, with its very sweetly-scented blooms. *C. armandii* and *C. cirrhosa* produce strands as long as 1 m (3½ ft). In the summer, and again in the autumn, there is a very wide choice of available clematis. Some particularly

delightful displays can be created by the herbaceous *C. × durandii*, with its striking flowers; *C. fusca* is viewed not so much for its beauty, but as a striking point of discussion; *C. recta* is worth growing for its 60–90 cm (2–3 ft) panicles of small white fragrant flowers; 'Huldine' is noteworthy for its semi-translucent white flower; and 'Henryi' for its stiff, sturdy stem. Other good large-flowered clematis are 'Barbara Jackman' 'Comtesse de Bouchaud', 'Gipsy Queen', 'Hagley Hybrid', 'Jackmanii', 'Kathleen Wheeler', 'Lawsoniana', 'Perle d'Azur', 'The President', 'Victoria', and 'W. E. Gladstone'. Double flowers stand out for their elegance, particularly 'Vyvyan Pennell' and *C. viticella* 'Purpurea Plena Elegans'.

A number of clematis have very attractive foliage. The unusual green leathery leaves of *C. armandii* can be effective with other flowers. *C. cirrhosa balearica* (*C. calycina*) has particularly fine, most delicate foliage.

There are also the considerable merits of clematis seed heads or fluffy heads for flower arranging. These can be used as they are, or they can be dried for winter display. Attractive seed heads can be obtained from *C. alpina*, *C. macropetala*, *C. orientalis*, *C. tangutica*, *C. serratifolia*, *C. fargesii*, *C. flammula* and *C. vitalba*.

The flowers can be displayed in a variety of ways. They can be shown on their own, maybe even a single bloom, or they can be displayed in conjunction with other flowers. A particularly pleasing way of displaying clematis flowers is with carefully matched roses. Usually the foliage used is the foliage of other plants.

The container should be carefully selected to match and enhance the beauty of that particular bloom. An unusual way of displaying clematis flowers is to cut the stem to a few centimetres (1 in) and allow the flower to rest in a bowl of water; patterns can vary with the selection of the coloured clematis. Long tresses can weep down or flow like a fountain from elevated vases. They can trail on window ledges or fall down from tall furniture.

For each ½ litre (1 pint) of water in the plant holder, a teaspoonful of sugar (as a nutrient) and ¼ teaspoonful of bleach (to kill bacteria) should be added. The flowers will last five to ten days. Should the clematis show signs of flopping, then 2.5 cm (1 in) should be cut off each stem and they should be put in water up to their necks overnight.

To obtain good strong stems, ie a bloom with a long peduncle, special attention has to be given to having healthy plants from which to collect the flowers. Thus every attention must be given to feeding. Particularly with the early-flowering large hybrids, care at pruning is of some importance; the stems should be pruned back to nearer the base than usual, to encourage the plant to put out strong growth. Those who have an abundance of glass can preserve areas in their greenhouses for producing strong plants for cutting.

Opposite:
A lovely combination of indigo-blue
C. × durandii *climbing into* Berberis
thunbergii *and framed by the yellow*
Senecio laxifolius.

CHAPTER THREE

CHOOSING THE BEST

The average gardener faced with a new plant would like to have recommended the well tried clematis and those of assured growth. In this list concentration is therefore on those clematis likely to have a universal appeal. There has to be, of course, room for individual choice; no two enthusiasts would agree exactly on the same list. Again, with more acquaintance, an enthusiasm may develop for one group of clematis. Furthermore, with increasing expertise, a gardener may be able to coax into bloom clematis of great fascination but of little vigour.

The following recommended list is divided into two groups: the large-flowered hybrids and the small-flowered species. It has now become traditional to group clematis in this way for description purposes. In the first group (Groups I(*b*) and II(*b*) of our classification outlined on page 19) the flowers can be truly large, like saucers, and spectacular. There can be many blooms, but they are unlikely to be as many as in the species. Some of the hybrids need considerable gardening attention. Some are liable to wilt. The small-flowered species (Groups I(*a*) and II(*a*) of our classification on page 19) are from the wild, or derived from plants in the wild. The flowers are small but there are many, many, flowers. The plants are usually vigorous and hardy. These are less liable to wilt than the large-flowered hybrids and more likely to be scented.

In each group the clematis appear alphabetically. The name appears first, with the common name in brackets if it has one. Then comes comment on habit and vigour. The height is given next, which can only be approximate as it will vary with conditions affecting the plant. This is followed by fairly detailed comment on the flower. The foliage comes next, followed by the pruning method, and lastly comment on noteworthy features of the clematis.

Time of flowering will be influenced by the position of your garden. The more northern the latitude in the northern hemisphere, or the more southerly in the southern hemisphere, the later clematis will flower. Again, the higher your garden from sea level, the later it will flower. Clematis on north walls will tend to flower later than on sunny south walls in the northern hemisphere and the reverse applies in the southern hemisphere.

Detailed information on pruning is given in Chapter 4. For pruning purposes, we now need to divide our two earlier mentioned groups (with their sub-divisions) into three groups of clematis. The first contains group I(*a*), the early-flowering species; the second is group I(*b*), consisting of the early-flowering large-flowered hybrids; and the third contains group II (*a* and *b*) including the late-flowering small-flowered species and the late-flowering large-flowered hybrids. Group I(*a*) requires little pruning except to be tidied into its allotted space after flowering, thus the term 'TIDY' is employed. Group I(*b*) requires a light trim before flowering and sometimes a light trim following flowering. Thus the term 'LIGHT' is employed here. Group II (*a* and *b*) requires hard pruning: these plants need to be cut close to the ground in late winter/early spring. Thus the term 'HARD' is employed here. Occasionally the term 'OPTIONAL' may be employed. For Group I(*b*) clematis 'optional' means that a plant can either have a trim, which means that it will flower early, or it can be pruned hard in which case the flowers will appear later. 'Optional' can also refer to Group II(*a* and *b*) clematis; no pruning means that the plant will flower early while the usual hard pruning means that the plant will flower later. (Consult Chapter 4 for more information.)

At first the gardener may be attracted to the spectacular large-flowered hybrids. Soon he begins to see the virtues of the

The spring-flowering 'Barbara Jackman' is a lovely example of a striped clematis. The petunia-mauve sepals have a striking crimson bar and contrast with the cream of the stamens.

small-flowered species. Anyone having more than a few clematis should experiment with the small-flowered species. Both the large-flowered and the small-flowered have different characteristics and complement one another. Certainly no-one would wish to be without a hardy macropetala and a hardy alpina early in the season, and later a montana for a mass effect, and a viticella for the early autumn. As a rule a chrysocoma will do as well as a montana. In the late season a herbaceous clematis can bring great interest to a border.

In the box below are found twelve easy to grow large-flowered clematis and twelve easy to grow small-flowered clematis. These approximate to the popularity lists of the International Clematis Society, published in Clematis International 1989.

With so many different species and hybrids available it can be difficult to know where to begin. The following short lists give a selection of clematis exhibiting particular characteristics. For those looking for especially notable blooms, then the first two lists below should help narrow the field. Clematis of a continuous-blooming habit are always good value in the garden. Also given are suggested hybrids where height, tall or short, is a prime consideration, species for the herbaceous border, those often tender but beautiful clematis, the evergreens, and those clematis noted for their scent. For good measure a list is included of intriguing, out of the ordinary clematis for gardeners who welcome a challenge. Details on all clematis mentioned are found in the descriptive lists beginning on page 65.

Easy to grow large-flowered hybrids

'Comtesse de Bouchaud' (pink), 'Dr Ruppel' (rose madder), 'Gipsy Queen' (purple), 'Hagley Hybrid' (pink), 'Jackmanii Alba' (white) 'Jackmanii Superba' (purple), 'Lasurstern' (blue), 'Marie Boisselot' (white), 'Mrs Cholmondeley' (lavender-blue), 'Nelly Moser' (striped), 'Perle d'Azur' (light blue), 'Victoria' (rosy purple).

Easy to grow small-flowered species

C. alpina 'Frances Rivis' (deep blue), C. alpina 'Ruby' (rosy red), C. chrysocoma (pale pink), C. flammula (white), C. integrifolia (purple-blue), C. macropetala (blue), C. macropetala 'Rosy O'Grady' (dark pink), C. montana 'Tetrarose' (lilac rose), C. orientalis 'Bill Mackenzie' (yellow), C. viticella 'Abundance' (pink), C. viticella 'Julia Correvon' (red), C. viticella 'Purpurea Plena Elegans' (dark purple).

Clematis with large blooms

'Belle Nantaise', 'Elsa Späth', 'Lawsoniana', 'Richard Pennell', 'W. E. Gladstone'. Large too, are 'Dr Ruppel', 'Kathleen Wheeler', 'Lasurstern' and 'Marie Boisselot'.

Double clematis

'Beauty of Worcester', 'Chalcedony', 'Daniel Deronda', 'Duchess of Edinburgh', 'Haku Ookan', 'Louise Rowe', 'Miss Crawshay', 'Mrs Spencer Castle', 'Proteus', 'Sylvia Denny', 'Vyvyan Pennell' (in my opinion the queen of clematis). An outstanding double viticella is C. viticella 'Purpurea Plena Elegans' – purple as the name suggests.

Continuous-blooming clematis

Exceptionally long bloomers are: 'Ascotiensis', 'Gipsy Queen', 'Lawsoniana', 'Mrs Cholmondeley', 'Perle d'Azur', 'The President', 'William Kennett', *C. × durandii*.

Tall-growing clematis hybrids

'Huldine', 'Lady Betty Balfour', 'Lawsoniana', 'Perle d'Azur', 'Star of India', 'Ville de Lyon', 'William Kennett'. Other tall growers are: 'Gipsy Queen', 'Jackmanii', 'Mrs Cholmondeley', 'W. E. Gladstone'.

Short-growing clematis

All alpinas and macropetalas, and the cultivars 'Alice Fisk', 'Barbara Jackman', 'Beauty of Worcester', 'Carnaby', 'Comtesse de Bouchaud', 'Dawn', 'Duchess of Edinburgh', *C. florida* 'Sieboldiana', 'Hagley Hybrid', 'Haku Ookan', 'Lady Northcliffe', 'Louise Rowe', Miss Bateman', 'Miss Crawshay', 'Moonlight', 'Mrs N. Thompson', 'Proteus'.

Herbaceous clematis

For a border a herbaceous clematis comes into its own.

C. addisonii, *C. × durandii*, *C. × eriostemon*, *C. heracleifolia* var. *davidiana*, *C. integrifolia*, *C. × jouiniana*, *C. recta*.

Evergreen clematis

Most clematis are deciduous but a few are evergreen.

C. armandii, *C. cirrhosa*, *C. cirrhosa* var. *balearica* (*C. calycina*), *C. forsteri*, *C. marmoraria*, *C. napaulensis*.

Fragrant clematis

Scent adds an extra dimension to a plant. In the list below it will be noticed that strong scent is a feature of the small-flowered species. Scent (in parentheses) is given when known.

C. afoliata (daphne-like), *C. armandii* (hawthorn), *C. × aromatica* (hawthorn-lemon), *C. chinensis* (strong), *C. cirrhosa* var. *balearica* (citrus), *C. crispa*, *C. flammula* (hawthorn), *C. forsteri* (lemon), *C. heracleifolia* var. *davidiana* 'Wyevale' (hyacinth), *C. integrifolia* 'Rosea', *C. maximowicziana* (hawthorn), *C. montana* 'Alexander' (strong), *C. montana* 'Elizabeth' (vanilla), *C. montana* 'Pictons Variety' (spicy), *C. montana* 'Tetrarose' (spicy), *C. montana* var. *rubens* (vanilla), *C. montana* 'Wilsonii' (chocolate), *C. recta* (strong, sweet), *C. rehderiana* (lemon or cowslips), *C. serratifolia* (lemon).

Out-of-the-ordinary clematis

Some readers may need to be introduced to the unusual, the special, the strange, the intriguing and the exotic. They are more effort but give more gain.

C. marmoraria (the smallest), *C. × durandii* (a lovely flower for the table), *C. florida* 'Sieboldiana' (exotic flower), *C. fusca* (surely not a clematis!), 'Vyvyan Pennell' (a paeony in the sky), *C. flammula* (for intense fragrance), *C. armandii* (thick, shiny, evergreen leaves), 'W. E. Gladstone' (the largest bloom of all), *C. cirrhosa* (for dead of winter), 'Perle d'Azur' (the world's sweetheart, it's No. 1).

Though short, 'Comtesse de Bouchaud' is an outstandingly popular clematis for its flood of bloom which lasts a long time. Easy to grow, it has mauve-pink tepals and cream stamens.

Large-flowered Hybrids

'Alice Fisk'
Moderately vigorous. Height to 2.4 m
(8 ft). Flower: 15–20 cm (6–8 in); eight
sepals; wisteria-blue sepals and purple
stamens. Flowers spring and early
autumn. Pruning – LIGHT. A short
clematis.

'Asao'
Moderately vigorous. Height to 2.4 m
(8 ft). Flowers: 15–20 cm (6–8 in); six to
seven sepals; reddish-pink sepals with
white bar and brown stamens. Flowers
early summer to early autumn. Pruning –
HARD. From Japan.

'Ascotiensis'
Vigorous. Height to 3.6 m (12 ft).
Flower: 15–20 cm (6–8 in); four to six
sepals; mauve-blue sepals and green
stamens. Flowers mid-summer to mid-
autumn continuously. Simple or heart
shaped, ternate leaves. Pruning – HARD.
Late flowerer.

'Barbara Jackman'
Vigorous. Height to 2.4 m (8 ft). Flower:
striped; 10 cm (4 in); eight sepals; petunia-
mauve sepals with crimson bars and
cream stamens; faint scent. Flowers late
spring to early summer. Leaves ternate.
Pruning – LIGHT. Early flowerer.

'Beauty of Worcester'
Moderately vigorous. Height 1.8 m (6 ft).
Flower: double in spring and single in
autumn; 12–15 cm (5–6 in); six sepals in
autumn flower; deep blue sepals and
white stamens. Flowers late spring and
early autumn. Single and ternate heart
shaped leaves. Pruning – LIGHT. Short

stemmed but grown for its early vivid
double flower.

'Bees Jubilee'
Not vigorous. Height to 2.4 m (8 ft).
Flower: striped; 18 cm (7 in); eight sepals;
mauve-pink sepals with carmine bars and
brown stamens. Flowers late spring and
early autumn. Leaves trifoliate. Pruning
– LIGHT. Flower often regarded as an
improved 'Nelly Moser'.

'Belle Nantaise'
Moderately vigorous. Height to 3 m
(10 ft). Flower: 20–25 cm (8–10 in); six
sepals; lavender-blue sepals and white
stamens. Flowers early summer to early
autumn. Leaves are simple and ternate.
Pruning – LIGHT. From France.

'Capitaine Thuilleaux'
Moderately vigorous. Height to 2.4 m
(8 ft). Flower: striped; 15–20 cm (6–8 in);
six to eight sepals; cream sepals with
strawberry-pink bars and brown stamens.
Flowers late spring and late summer.
Leaves ternate. Pruning – LIGHT. From
France.

'Carnaby'
Vigorous. Height to 2.4 m (8 ft). Flower:
striped; 15–20 cm (6–8 in); six sepals;
raspberry-pink sepals with deeper bar and
brown stamens. Flowers late spring.
Pruning – LIGHT.

'Chalcedony'
Vigorous. Height to 2.4 m (8 ft). Flower:
double in spring and autumn; 12 cm
(5 in); 50–60 sepals in a ball; ice-blue
sepals and creamy stamens. Flowers late
spring and early autumn. Solitary and ternate leathery leaves. Pruning – LIGHT.

'Charissima'
Vigorous. Height to 3.6 m (12 ft). Flower: striped; 18 cm (7 in); eight sepals; cerise-pink with maroon bar and maroon stamens. Flowers early summer. Leaves are ternate. Pruning – LIGHT.

'Comtesse de Bouchaud'
Very vigorous and free flowering. Height to 2.4 m (8 ft). Flower: 10–15 cm (4–6 in); six sepals; sepals are mauve-pink with cream stamens. Flowers continuously early summer to early autumn. Leaves have three to five leaflets. Pruning – HARD. Outstanding, very popular, pink clematis. Very free flowering but short. In top ten of International Clematis Society list. From France.

'Daniel Deronda'
Moderately vigorous. Height to 3 m (10 ft). Flower: semi-double or single; 18–20 cm (7–8 in); eight sepals; violet-blue sepals and creamy stamens. Flowers late spring. Simple and ternate leaves. Pruning – LIGHT. Has a double bloom in the spring and a single bloom in the autumn.

'Dawn'
Moderately vigorous. Height to 1.8 m (6 ft). Flower: 15–20 cm (6–8 in); eight sepals; sepals are pearly-pink with carmine stamens. Flowers late spring; slight scent. Leaves are ternate. Pruning – LIGHT. Tends to fade.

'Dr Ruppel'
Very vigorous and free flowering. Height to 3 m (10 ft). Flower: striped; 15–20 cm (4–6 in); eight sepals; rose-madder sepals with brilliant carmine bar and golden stamens. Flowers freely late spring and early autumn. The leaves are solitary and ternate. Pruning – LIGHT. Outstanding for its colour and free flowering habit. Very popular since its introduction from Argentina in 1975. Best striped clematis. In top ten of International Clematis Society List.

'Duchess of Edinburgh'
Not vigorous. Height to 2.4 m (8 ft). Flower: double; 10 cm (4 in); rows of white sepals with cream stamens; sometimes sepals have green tinge; faint smell. Flowers early to late summer. Leaves ternate. Pruning – LIGHT. A white double.

'Elsa Späth' (syn. 'Xerxes')
Very vigorous and free flowering. Height to 2 m (7 ft). Flower: 20 cm (8 in); six to eight sepals; lavender-blue sepals and reddish-purple stamens. Flowers early summer and again in early autumn. Three to five leaflets. Pruning – LIGHT. A fine reliable clematis.

'Ernest Markham'
Vigorous. Height to 3.5 m (12 ft). Flower: 10–15 cm (4–6 in); six sepals; sepals petunia-red with golden stamens. Flowers mid-summer to mid-autumn. Leaves have three or five leaflets. Pruning – either LIGHT for early display and HARD for late display. A popular red clematis.

'Fair Rosamond'
Moderately vigorous. Height to 2.4 m (8 ft). Flower: striped; 12–15 cm (5–6 in); eight sepals; sepals are bluish-white with red bars and purple stamens. Flowers early summer; scent of violets. Ternate leaves. Pruning – LIGHT. The only large-flowered hybrid with fair scent.

'General Sikorski'
Vigorous. Height to 2.4 m (8 ft). Flower: 15–20 cm (6–8 in); six sepals; mid-blue and crenulated edges to sepals with golden stamens. Flowers continuously from early summer to autumn. Pruning – LIGHT. An exceptional recent introduction from Poland which will become very popular.

'Gipsy Queen'
Very vigorous. Height to 3.6 m (12 ft). Flower: 10–15 cm (4–6 in); six sepals and reddish-purple stamens. Flowers continuously from mid-summer to early autumn. Ternate leaves. Pruning – HARD. Outstanding for ease of cultivation and continuous free flowering.

'Hagley Hybrid'
Very vigorous. Height to 1.8 m (6 ft). Flower: 10–15 cm (4–6 in); six sepals; shell-pink sepals and brown stamens. Flowers continuously early summer to early autumn. Leaves are ternate. Pruning – HARD. Despite short height, is very popular for its continuous free flowering nature, and ease of cultivation.

'Haku Ookan'
Moderately vigorous. Height to 2.4 m (8 ft). Flower: semi-double in spring; 15–20 cm (6–8 in); eight sepals; violet sepals and white stamens. Flowers early summer and again in early autumn. Ternate leaves. Pruning – LIGHT. From Japan.

'Henryi'
Moderately vigorous. Height to 3 m (10 ft). Flower: 15–20 cm (6–8 in); eight sepals; creamy-white sepals and brown stamens. Flowers early summer to early autumn. Ternate leaves. Pruning – LIGHT. One of the oldest hybrid clematis and comes from Scotland.

'H. F. Young'
Vigorous and free flowering. Height to 3.6 m (12 ft). Flower: 15–20 cm (6–8 in); Wedgwood blue sepals and creamy-white stamens. Flowers late spring and early summer. Ternate leaves. Pruning – LIGHT. Exceptional. One of the best blue clematis and very popular for free flowering habit. Likes sun.

'Horn of Plenty'
Moderately vigorous. Height to 3.6 m (12 ft) Flower: 15–20 cm (6–8 in); eight sepals; rosy-purple sepals and reddish-purple stamens. Flowers early summer to early autumn. Leaves ternate. Pruning – HARD.

'Huldine'
Very vigorous and free flowering. Height to 6 m (20 ft). Flower: 5–10 cm (2–4 in); six sepals; sepals pearly-white and greenish-white stamens. Flowers continuously early summer to mid-autumn. Five leaflets. Pruning – HARD. This white clematis is very popular for its free flowering habit.

'Jackmanii Alba'
Very vigorous. Height 6 m (20 ft). Flower: 10–12 cm (4–5 in); semi-double at first with six sepals later; white sepals and brown stamens. Flowers continuously early summer to early autumn. Ternate light green leaves. Pruning – HARD. Easy to grow.

'Jackmanii Superba'
Very vigorous and free flowering. Height

to 6 m (20 ft). Flower: 10–15 cm (4–6 in); sepals 4–6; bluish-purple sepals and greenish beige stamens. Flowers continuously early summer to early autumn. Leaves simple, ternate, or in fives. Pruning – HARD. Outstanding for continuous flowering, colour, free flowering habit, and ease of cultivation. An improved 'Jackmanii'. In top ten of International Clematis Society list.

'Jan Pawel II' ('John Paul II')
Vigorous. Height to 5 m (16 ft). Flowers: 15–20 cm (6–8 in); creamy-white sepals with pink shading and brown stamens. Flowers late spring and early autumn. Pruning – LIGHT. From Poland.

'Kathleen Wheeler'
Vigorous. Height to 2.4 m (8 ft). Flower: 20–25 cm (8–10 in); eight sepals; plummy-mauve sepals and golden stamens. Flowers early summer and early autumn. Leaves simple or ternate. Pruning – LIGHT.

'Lady Betty Balfour'
Vigorous. Height to 6 m (20 ft). Flower: 15–20 cm (6–8 in); six sepals; violet-blue sepals with yellow stamens. Flowers early and mid-autumn. Leaves are ternate. Pruning – HARD. Valuable for late flowering and therefore needs sunny position.

'Lady Northcliffe'
Vigorous. Height 1.8 m (6 ft). Flowers: 10–15 cm (4–6 in); six sepals; deep Wedgwood-blue sepals and white stamens. Flowers continuously early summer to mid-autumn. Leaves are ternate. Pruning – LIGHT. Popular for continuous flowering.

'Lasurstern'
Vigorous. Height to 3.6 m (12 ft). Flower: 17–22 cm (7–9 in); handsome flower with rich deep blue sepals and white stamens. Flowers profusely late spring and some flowers in early autumn. Leaves are ternate. Pruning – LIGHT. Outstanding clematis and in top ten of International Clematis Society list.

'Lawsoniana'
Vigorous. Height to 5 m (16 ft). Flower: 20–25 cm (8–10 in); six to eight sepals; lavender-blue sepals with rosy tinge and beige stamens. Flowers early summer to late autumn. Leaves are ternate. Pruning – LIGHT. One of the oldest clematis, from Scotland. Exceptional for vigour, height and length of flowering.

'Lincoln Star'
Not vigorous. Height to 2 m (6 ft). Flower: 15–20 cm (6–8 in); eight sepals; sepals are cochineal-pink with paler margins and maroon stamens. Flowers late spring and early autumn. Leaves are ternate. Pruning – LIGHT.

'Louise Rowe'
Not vigorous. Height to 2.4 m (8 ft). Flower: unusual – single, semi-double, and double flowers at same time; 10–15 cm (4–6 in); pale mauve sepals and golden stamens. Flowering early summer and again early autumn. Pruning –

Opposite:
'Elsa Späth' is sometimes known as 'Xerxes'. A vigorous and reliable clematis that gives a big crop of flowers in early summer and again in early autumn.

The spring-blooming 'Lasurstern' is justifiably popular for the handsome deep blue tepals that contrast with the white stamens to make a striking flower. Vigorous and free flowering.

LIGHT. Bred by an amateur gardener. A curiosity, but tricky.

'Mme Baron Veillard'

Vigorous. Height to 3.6 m (12 ft). Flower: 10–15 cm (4–6 in); six sepals; lilac-rose sepals with white stamens. Flowers continuously mid- to late autumn. Leaves are ternate. Pruning – HARD. Useful as a vigorous late-flowering clematis. From France.

'Mme Edouard André'

Moderately vigorous. Height to 2.4 m (8 ft). Flower: 10–15 cm (4–6 in); six sepals; wine red sepals and cream stamens. Flowers continuously early summer to early autumn. Leaves are ternate. Pruning – HARD. A popular red from France.

'Mme Julia Correvon'

Very vigorous and free flowering. Height to 2.4 m (8 ft). Flower: 5–10 cm (2–4 in); four to six sepals; deep wine-red sepals and golden stamens. Flowers continuously early summer to early autumn. Five leaflets. Pruning – HARD. This popular free-flowering red is from the viticella group and is here because of large blooms. From France.

'Margaret Hunt'

Vigorous. Height to 3.5 m (12 ft). Flower: 10–15 cm (4–6 in); lavender-pink sepals and brown stamens. Flowers continuously early summer to early autumn. Pruning – HARD. Bred by an amateur gardener and named after her.

'Margot Koster'

Vigorous and free flowering. Height to 2.4 m (8 ft). Flower: 5–10 cm (2–4 in); four to six sepals; mauve-pink sepals and whitish stamens. Flowers mid-summer continuously. Five leaflets. Pruning – HARD. From the viticella group and appears here for size of bloom.

'Marie Boisselot' (syn. 'Mme Le Coultre')

Very vigorous. Height to 5 m (16 ft). Flower: 15–20 cm (6–8 in); eight sepals; pure white sepals and pale yellow stamens. Flowers continuously early summer to early autumn. Leaves simple or ternate. Pruning – LIGHT. This outstanding clematis from France is the best white clematis. In top ten of International Clematis Society list.

'Miss Bateman'

Vigorous. Height to 2.4 m (8 ft). Flower: 10–15 cm (4–6 in); eight sepals; creamy-white sepals and chocolate-red stamens. Flowers late spring and again early autumn. Leaves are ternate. Pruning – LIGHT. Attractive early flower.

'Miss Crawshay'

Moderately vigorous. Height to 1.8 m (6 ft). Flower: semi-double in first blooming; 10–15 cm (4–6 in); eight sepals, mauve-pink sepals and pale fawn stamens. Flowers late spring. Leaves are ternate. Pruning – LIGHT.

'Moonlight' (syn. 'Wada's Primrose', 'Yellow Queen').

Not vigorous. Height to 2.4 m (8 ft). Flower: 10–15 cm (6–8 in); eight sepals; soft primrose sepals and yellow stamens. Flowers late spring and early autumn. Leaves are ternate. Pruning – LIGHT. Pretty flower needing shade.

'Mrs Cholmondeley'

Very vigorous and free flowering. Height to 5 m (16 ft). Flower: 18–23 cm (7–9 in); six or seven sepals; lavender-blue sepals and brown stamens. Flowers for a long period late spring to early autumn. Three or five leaflets. Pruning – LIGHT. 'Mrs "Chumley"' is very popular for its trouble-free long flowering.

'Mrs N. Thompson'

Moderately vigorous. Height to 2 m (6 ft) or less. Flower: striped; 10–15 cm (4–6 in); four to six sepals; deep violet-blue sepals with vivid scarlet bar and deep red stamens. Flowers late spring and early autumn. Pruning – LIGHT. Has to be grown for its gorgeously coloured flower.

'Mrs P. B. Truax'

Moderately vigorous. Height to 3.6 m (12 ft). Flower: silky texture; 10–15 cm (4–6 in); eight sepals; periwinkle-blue sepals and yellow stamens. Flowers late spring and early autumn. Leaves are ternate. Pruning – LIGHT.

'Mrs Spencer Castle'

Moderately vigorous. Height to 3.6 m (12 ft). Flower: double flowers in first blooming; 10–15 cm (4–6 in); six sepals; heliotrope-pink sepals with golden stamens. Flowers late spring and early autumn. Leaves are ternate. Pruning – LIGHT.

'Myojo'

Moderately vigorous. Height to 2.4 m (8 ft). Flower: 10–15 cm (4–6 in); velvety violet-red sepals with deeper bar and cream stamens. Flowers late spring and early autumn. Pruning – LIGHT. From Japan.

'Nelly Moser'

Very vigorous. Height to 2.4 m (8 ft). Flower: striped; 18–23 cm (7–9 in); eight sepals; pale mauve-pink sepals with deep carmine bars and maroon stamens. Flowers late spring and early autumn. Leaves are ternate. Pruning – LIGHT. Justifiably popular for its free flowering but needs shade to prevent fading.

'Niobe'

Vigorous. Height to 2.4 m (8 ft). Flower: velvety; 10–15 cm (4–6 in); deep ruby-red sepals and golden stamens making an exceptional bloom. Flowers continuously early summer to early autumn. Leaves are ternate. Pruning – HARD. Outstanding recent introduction from Poland. In top ten of International Clematis Society list.

'Perle d'Azur'

Very vigorous and free flowering. Height to 5 m (16 ft). Flower: 10–15 cm (4–6 in); four to six sepals; sky-blue sepals with green stamens. Flowers continuously early summer to mid-autumn. The leaves are ternate or in fives. Pruning – HARD. Raised in France. For its beautiful blue colour, continuous blooming and vigour, it topped the International Clematis Society list.

'The President'

Vigorous and free flowering. Height to 3 m (10 ft). Flower: 15–20 cm (6–8 in); eight sepals; deep purple-blue sepals and reddish-purple stamens. Flowers continuously from early summer to early autumn. The leaves are ternate. Pruning – LIGHT. Outstanding clematis for its vigour and continuous blooming. In top ten of International Clematis Society list.

'Marie Boisselot', sometimes known as 'Mme Le Coultre' – the latter became her married name is the best white clematis for its beauty and vigour. Float the enormous white blooms on water for a magical effect.

'Prince Charles'
Moderately vigorous. Height to 2.4 m (8 ft). Flower: 10–15 cm (4–6 in); mauve-blue sepals and green stamens. Flowers early summer to early autumn. Pruning – HARD. Recent introduction from New Zealand.

'Proteus'
Moderately vigorous. Height to 2.4 m (8 ft). Flower: double or treble at first; 15–20 cm (6–8 in); six sepals; rosy-lilac sepals and yellow stamens. Flowers early summer to early autumn. The leaves are ternate. Pruning – LIGHT. Very old clematis and a double.

'Ramona' (syn. 'Hybrida Sieboldiana')
Moderately vigorous. Height to 5 m (16 ft). Flower: 15–20 cm (6–8 in); lavender-blue sepals and dark stamens. Flowers early summer to early autumn. Pruning – LIGHT.

'Richard Pennell'
Very vigorous and free flowering. Height to 2.4 m (8 ft). Flower: 15–20 cm (6–8 in); eight sepals; rosy-purple sepals and golden stamens. Flowers continuously late spring to early autumn. Leaves are ternate. Pruning – LIGHT. An exceptional post war hybrid, likely to become increasingly popular.

Opposite:
Early-flowering 'Miss Bateman' is an excellent example of the striking effect produced by contrasting central stamens, here chocolate-red, and tepals, here creamy-white.

'Rouge Cardinal'
Not vigorous. Height to 2.4 m (8 ft). Flower: 10–15 cm (4–6 in); six sepals; ruby-red sepals and brown stamens. Flowers early summer to early autumn. Leaves are ternate. Pruning – LIGHT. From France.

'Scartho Gem'
Not vigorous. Height to 1.8 m (6 ft). Flower: 15–20 cm (6–8 in); eight sepals; bright deep pink sepals and golden stamens. Flowers early summer to early autumn. The leaves are ternate. Pruning – LIGHT.

'Serenata'
Vigorous. Height to 3.6 m (12 ft). Flower: 10–15 cm (4–6 in); purple sepals and yellow stamens. Flowers late spring continuously to early autumn. Pruning – HARD. From Sweden.

'Sylvia Denny'
Vigorous. Height to 2.4 m (8 ft). Flower: double early on; 10–15 cm (4–6 in); white sepals and yellow stamens; said to have a slight scent. Flowers late spring and early autumn. Pruning – LIGHT. Recent introduction from England.

'Twilight'
Vigorous. Height to 2.4 m (8 ft). Flower: 15–20 cm (6–8 in); six sepals; petunia-mauve, slightly fluorescent sepals and yellow stamens. Flowers continuously mid-summer to mid-autumn. Leaves simple or ternate. Pruning – HARD.

'Victoria'
Very vigorous and free flowering. Height to 3 m (16 ft). Flower: 10–15 cm (4–6 in); four to six sepals; rosy-purple sepals and

buff stamens. Flowers continuously early summer to early autumn. Leaflets in fives. Pruning – HARD. Popular for free-flowering habit and has a reputation for withstanding cold climates. In top ten of International Clematis Society list.

'Ville de Lyon'

Very vigorous. Height to 3.6 m (12 ft). Flower: 10–15 cm (4–6 in); six sepals, carmine red sepals and golden stamens. Flowers continuously from mid-summer to mid-autumn. Leaflets three or five. Pruning – HARD. Raised in France. In top ten of the International Clematis Society list for its vigour.

'Vyvyan Pennell'

Vigorous. Height to 2.4 m (8 ft). Flower: double at first, single later; paeony-like flower; 12–20 cm (6–8 in); deep violet-blue sepals suffused with purple and red and golden stamens. Flowers late spring and early autumn. Leaves are ternate. Pruning – LIGHT. The best double clematis. Outstanding. Grow this clematis so that you can gaze into the kaleidoscope of fascinating shades of blue in this paeony-like flower. Queen of the clematis.

'W. E. Gladstone'

Vigorous. Height to 3.6 m (12 ft). Flower: 20–25 cm (8–10 in); six or seven sepals; lilac-blue sepals and purple stamens. Flowers early summer to mid-autumn. Leaves are simple or ternate. Pruning – LIGHT. The largest blooms of all and has been very long in cultivation. Dislikes winter but always jumps up again. Will even bloom on a north wall and often chosen for this purpose.

'William Kennett'

Vigorous. Height to 3.6 m (12 ft). Flower: 15–20 cm (6–8 in); eight sepals; deep lavender-blue, crinkly sepals with dark purple stamens. Flowers continuously early summer to early autumn. Solitary leaves. Pruning – LIGHT. A very old clematis and still popular for its height and vigour, despite being described in the first English clematis book as 'wanting in refinement'.

Small-flowered Species

C. addisonii (named after Addison, presumably an American)

Moderately vigorous but needs protection. Height to 38 cm (15 in). Flower: pitcher shaped; 2.5 cm (1 in) long; four fleshy sepals; rosy-purple sepals and cream stamens. Flowers early summer. Leaves are solitary. Pruning – HARD. A short herbaceous clematis from the USA.

C. afoliata (rush-stemmed clematis)

Moderately vigorous; needs protection. Male and female plants. Height to 2.4 m (8 ft). Flower: tubular; 1.2–1.8 cm $\frac{1}{2}$–$\frac{3}{4}$ in); four sepals; pale yellow sepals; daphne scent. Flowers late spring. Three leaflets. Pruning – TIDY. An untidy, tender, interesting clematis from New Zealand, suitable for borders.

Opposite:
'Mrs Cholmondeley' is everyone's darling for its reliability, mass of bloom, and its continuous flowering. Trouble free, it has lavender-blue tepals and brown stamens.

C. alpina (the alpine virgin's bower)
Vigorous, hardy, and easy to grow.
Height to 2.4 m (8 ft). Flower: nodding
bells; 4 cm (1½ in); four sepals with
staminodes between sepals and stamens;
lavender blue sepals; white staminodes.
Flowers mid-spring. Leaves are double
ternate. Pruning – TIDY. First clematis to
appear in spring. Excellent for north-
facing walls and scrambling over rocks,

*'Niobe' is an outstanding introduction from
Poland. The deep red velvety tepals and the
golden stamens make a handsome,
eyecatching flower. It has become extremely
popular.*

tree stumps, etc. A number of varieties
are available:
C. a. 'Burford White' – white; C. a.

'Columbine' – pale blue; *C. a.* 'Frances Rivis' – deep blue (largest flower); *C. a.* 'Jacqueline du Pré' – mauve-pink (very vigorous); *C. a.* 'Pamela Jackman' – mid-blue; *C. a.* 'Ruby' – rosy-red; *C. a.* 'Rosy Pagoda' – pale pink; *C. a.* 'Sibirica' – creamy-white; *C. a.* 'White Moth' – double white. The alpinas are high up the table in the International Clematis Society list.

C. armandii (Armand's clematis)
Very vigorous on warm wall. Height to 9 cm (30 ft). Flower: in clusters; 5 cm (2 in) across; four to six sepals; sepals are white with yellow stamens; conspicuous vanilla fragrance. Flowers mid-spring. Variety 'Apple Blossom' is pale pink, and 'Snowdrift' is pure white. Evergreen. Large dark green leathery ternate leaves. Pruning – TIDY. This Chinese clematis is grown for its delicious scent in spring and handsome foliage. Needs plenty of room. In the top ten of the International Clematis Society list.

C. chrysocoma (the hairy clematis)
Very vigorous and hardy. Height to 6 m (20 ft). Flower: cup shaped; 6 cm (2½ in); four sepals; sepals pale pink and creamy stamens. Flowers late spring. Young shoots and leaves covered with golden hairy down. Ternate leaves. Pruning – TIDY. This Chinese clematis is akin to a montana but more desirable as less rampant.

C. cirrhosa (the tendril clematis)
Vigorous on a warm wall. Height to 4 m (15 ft). Flower: bell shaped; 4–5 cm (1½–2 in); four sepals; creamy-white sepals with no freckles. Flowers early winter to mid-spring. Tri-lobed ovate leaves. Pruning – TIDY. Very similar to, but not as popular as, *C. cirrhosa* var. *balearica* – no freckles and no fern-like leaves.

C. cirrhosa var. *balearica* (syn. *C. calycina*) (the fern-leaved clematis)
Vigorous on sheltered wall. Height to 6 m (20 ft). Flower: bell shaped; 4–5 cm (1½–2 in); four sepals; yellow-white sepals with reddish-maroon freckles. Flowers early winter to mid-spring. Scented – citrus. Evergreen; fern-like. Pruning – TIDY. From the Balearic islands. Can easily be confused with *C. cirrhosa*, which is less vigorous. Ideal under glass if room available.

C. crispa (the curly clematis)
Moderately vigorous. Height to 1.5 m (5 ft). Flower: bell shaped; 4–5 cm (1–1½ in); four sepals; sepals are pale blue with cream stamens; scented. Flowers early summer to early autumn. Five to seven leaflets. Pruning – HARD. From the United States.

C. × *durandii* (Durand's clematis)
Vigorous and free flowering herbaceous type. Height to 1.2 m (4 ft). Flower: 10–15 cm (4–6 in); four to six sepals; indigo-blue sepals and yellow-white stamens. Flowers continuously mid-summer to mid-autumn. The leaves are solitary. Pruning – HARD. Like a sub-shrub. Lovely flower for cutting.

C. × *eriostemon* 'Hendersonii'
Vigorous, hardy, semi-herbaceous type. Height to 2.4 m (8 ft). Flower: nodding bell; 5 cm (2 in); four sepals; blue-purple sepals and green-yellow stamens. Flowers mid-summer to mid-autumn. The leaves

are simple. Pruning – HARD. True to its herbaceous nature, it dies down to the ground in winter.

C. fargesii var. souliei (Farges's clematis)

Vigorous. 7.5 m (25 ft). Flower: in threes; 5–7.5 cm (2–3 in); six sepals; sepals are white with greenish-white stamens. Flowers continuously early summer to early autumn. Hairy, two or three-lobed leaves. Pruning – HARD. A Chinese clematis said to grow well in cold climates.

C. flammula (clematis of a little flame or star, or the fragrant Virgin's bower)

Very vigorous. Height to 6 m (20 ft). Flower: cruciform and produced in abundance; 2.4–4 cm (1–1½ in); four sepals; white sepals and white stamens; hawthorn scent. Flowers late summer to mid-autumn. Biternate leaves. Pruning – OPTIONAL. Exceptional south European clematis for a scented mass effect in autumn. In top ten of International Clematis Society list.

C. florida 'Sieboldiana' (syn. C.f. 'Bicolor')

Not vigorous and needs protected environment. Height to 3 m (10 ft). Flower: dramatic; 10 cm (4 in); five or six sepals; sepals are greenish-white with purple prominent stamens. Flowers early summer to early autumn. Five leaflets. Pruning – LIGHT. This Japanese plant is eye-catching (same effect as passion flower), but tricky to grow.

C. forsteri

Not vigorous and needs protection. Height to 3.6 m (12 ft). Flower: numerous; 1.8 cm (¾ in); five to eight sepals; sepals are greenish-yellow with golden stamens; lemon scent. Flowers early summer. Evergreen. Ternate leaves. Pruning – TIDY. Tender New Zealand evergreen.

C. fusca (dark-coloured clematis)

Vigorous and hardy. Height to 3.6 m (12 ft). Flower: unusual; urn shaped; four sepals, 2 cm (¾ in); thick sepals are purple but covered with dark brown hairs, a pale green inside, and with cream stamens. Flowers mid-summer. Leaves have five to nine leaflets. Pruning – HARD. A curiosity from Asia. Most unclematis-like. An arresting cut flower.

C. heracleifolia var. davidiana

Vigorous herbaceous plant. Height to 90 cm (3 ft). Flower: in dense clusters like a hyacinth; 4 cm (1½ in); four to six sepals; lavender-blue sepals; very scented. Flowers mid-summer. Ternate leaves. Pruning – HARD. Good bushy clematis from China. Variety 'Wyevale' is an 'improved' version of above, with more prominent yellow stamens.

C. integrifolia (simple leaf clematis, or Hungarian clematis)

Vigorous herbaceous type. Height to 60 cm (2 ft). Flower: nodding bell; 2.5 cm (1 in); four sepals; purple-blue sepals and creamy stamens. Flowers mid-summer. Leaves simple. Pruning – HARD. This clematis is the best known herbaceous clematis and in top ten of International Clematis Society list. Variety 'Olgae' is larger, a clear blue and scented; 'Pastel Blue' is larger, light blue and scented; 'Rosea', with bright pink colouring and scented, is outstanding.

Long-flowering 'Richard Pennell' has made an impact with its handsome flowers and vigorous free-flowering habit. It has rosy-purple tepals and golden stamens.

'Vyvyan Pennell' is surely the queen of the clematis. The paeony-like flower is a kaleidoscope of fascinating shades of violet, purple and red. The best double clematis, giving a bonus of single flowers in the autumn.

C. ×jouiniana 'Praecox' (after the Frenchman, Jouin)

Vigorous and free flowering. Height to 3 m (10 ft). Flower: 4–5 cm (1½–2 in); four to six sepals; bluish-white sepals. Flowers in mid-summer to mid-autumn. Three to

five leaflets. Golden yellow in autumn.
Pruning – HARD. Useful tumbling down
a bank or scrambling over a conifer
bed.

C. macropetala (large-petalled, or the downy clematis)

Very vigorous and hardy. Height to 4.5 m
(15 ft). Flower: double, nodding bell;
6–8 cm (2½–3 in); sepals and outer
staminodes are lavender-blue and inner
staminodes are white; flowering mid- and
late spring. Young shoots covered with
down. Biternate leaves. Pruning – TIDY.
Outstanding Asian clematis. Has to be
grown for joyfulness in spring. High up
in the top ten of the International
Clematis Society list. Will stand shade
and a north wall. Variety 'Bluebird' is a
deep blue; 'Markham's Pink' is a lovely
pink; and 'Rosy O'Grady', a darker pink,
is very popular.

C. marmoraria (of marble)

Vigorous low sub-shrub grown as alpine.
Height to 6 cm (3¼ in). Flower: male
2–3 cm (¾–1 in), female 1.6–2.4 cm
(½–1 in); sepals white. Flowers in spring.
Leathery, hairy, leaves. Pruning – TIDY.
From New Zealand. Smallest known
clematis, an attractive curiosity and a
'must' for rockery enthusiasts.

C. maximowicziana (after the curator of the Leningrad Botanical Institute) (syn. C. paniculata)

Very vigorous. Height to 9 m (30 ft).
Flower: cruciform; 3 cm (1¼ in); white
sepals, hawthorn scented; flowering early
and mid-autumn. Three to five leaflets.
Pruning – OPTIONAL. A Japanese
late-flowering option to *C. flammula*.

C. montana (the mountain clematis or Indian virgin's bower)

Very vigorous but not for cold climates.
Height to 9 m (30 ft) and above in some
varieties. Flower: in profusion; 5 cm
(2 in); four sepals; sepals are white with
pale-cream stamens. Flowers for a short
period in late spring. Some varieties are
scented. Ternate leaves. Pruning – TIDY.
This Himalayan clematis is ideal for a
mass effect in spring where there is plenty
of room. In top ten of International
Clematis Society list. A large number of
varieties exist, including *C.m.*
'Alexander' – white, scented, slow to
start; C.m. 'Elizabeth' – pale pink,
vanilla scent; *C.m.* 'Grandiflora' – larger
white bloom, most vigorous of all
clematis, no scent; *C. m.* 'Mayleen' –
large deep pink flowers, bronze foliage,
scented; *C. m.* 'Pink Perfection' – deep
pink, scented; *C. m.* 'Tetrarose' – lilac
rose, large flower, scented, bronze
foliage; *C. m.* 'Wilsonii' – creamy, scent
of hot chocolate, flowers later than
others.

C. napaulensis (the Nepal clematis) (syn. C. forrestii)

Not vigorous and needs protection.
Height to 7.5 m (25 ft). Flower: bell-
shaped clusters; 3 cm (1¼ in); four sepals
are 2 cm (¾ in) long and stamens 3 cm
(1¼ in); creamy white sepals and
protruding maroon stamens. Flowers
mid-winter. Semi-evergreen. Ternate
leaves. Pruning – TIDY. A Himalayan
clematis which makes a winter curiosity
for those with abundant glass.

C. orientalis (oriental clematis)

Vigorous but likes sun. Height to 6 m

(20 ft). Flower: usually opening wide or recurved; 5 cm (2 in); four sepals; yellow sepals and brown stamens. Flowers mid-summer to mid-autumn. Prominent seed heads. Finely cut foliage. Prune – OPTIONAL. This late-flowering clematis is very popular for its yellow colouring and seed heads. In top ten of the International Clematis Society list. There are two outstanding varieties – L&S No. 13342 (orange peel clematis) with thick fleshy sepals and 'Bill Mackenzie', with largest flowers, up to 8 cm (3 in).

C. recta (the straight clematis)

Vigorous herbaceous type. Height to 1.5 m (4 ft). Flower: panicles of bloom; cruciform; 1.8–3 cm ($\frac{3}{4}$–$1\frac{1}{2}$ in); white sepals. Flowers mid-summer; scented. Five to six leaflets. Pruning – HARD. This European clematis can make a good bush in the border.

C. rehderiana (Rehder's clematis, or the nodding virgin's bower)

Vigorous but needs sun. Height to 6 m (20 ft). Flower: in panicles; nodding bells; 1.2 cm ($\frac{1}{2}$ in); four sepals; primrose-yellow sepals. Flowers late summer to mid-autumn; cowslip scent. Five to nine leaflets. Pruning – OPTIONAL. Interesting Chinese curiosity for late summer.

C. serratifolia (cut-leaf clematis)

Vigorous and free flowering. Needs sun. Height to 3.5 m (12 ft). Flower: open bell; 4–5 cm ($1\frac{1}{2}$–2 in; four sepals; primrose-yellow sepals and purple stamens; lemon-scented; seed heads. Flowers late summer and early autumn. Biternate leaves. Pruning – OPTIONAL. From Korea.

C. spooneri (syn. C. chrysocoma var. sericea)

Very vigorous and free flowering. Height to 9 cm (30 ft). Flower: clustered; 8 cm (3 in); four sepals; white sepals and yellow stamens; no scent. Flowers late spring. Ternate downy leaves. Pruning – TIDY. Similar to montanas and chrysocoma, superior in size of white flowers, but lacking scent.

C. tangutica 'Gravetye' (from Tangut, Tibet)

Very vigorous. Height to 6 m (20 ft). Flower: bell- or lantern-shaped; 2.5–4 cm (1–$1\frac{1}{2}$ in); four sepals; yellow sepals and brownish stamens; seed heads. Flowers mid-summer to mid-autumn. Five to seven leaflets. Pruning – HARD. Easily confused with *C. orientalis*; it is from the same sub-group but said to have better seed heads and flowers more lantern-shaped. Nevertheless in top ten of the International Clematis Society list.

C. texensis (the Texan clematis) (syn. C. coccinea) 'Duchess of Albany'

Vigorous semi-herbaceous plant. Height to 2.4 m (8 ft). Flower: pitcher or urn-shaped; 2.5 cm (1 in); four to six sepals; fleshy pink sepals with rose-pink bars and cream stamens. Flowers late summer to mid-autumn. Three to five heart-shaped leaflets. Pruning – HARD. American. Related varieties are: 'Etoile Rose', cerise-pink with sepals edged in silver; 'Gravetye Beauty', crimson sepals and red stamens; 'Sir Trevor Lawrence', deep carmine sepals and cream stamens. All the texensis are outstanding for their showy, intriguing blooms. In the top ten of the International Clematis Society list.

'W. E. Gladstone' not only has handsome flowers but produces enormous blooms, the largest of all clematis. Compare its size with the outstretched hand behind.

C. × vedrariensis

Vigorous. Height to 6 m (20 ft). Flower: cup shaped; 7–8 cm (3 in); four to six sepals; sepals rosy-mauve; Flowers late spring. Golden hairs on shoots and young leaves. Ternate leaves. Pruning – TIDY. A cross between *C. chrysocoma* and *C. montana* var. *rubens*.

C. viticella (the purple virgin's bower)

Very vigorous, hardy and free flowering. Height to 6 m (12 ft). Flower: saucer shaped; 4–6 cm (1½–2½ in); four sepals; purple sepals and green stamens. Flowers mid-summer to early autumn. Five to seven leaflets. Pruning – HARD. This clematis is usually grown in one of the following forms: *C. v.* 'Abundance' – striking pink-red sepals with creamy green stamens; *C. v.* 'Alba Luxurians' – creamy white sepals with green tips and creamy-green stamens; *C. v.* 'Etoile Violette' – large blooms, purple sepals and creamy-yellow stamens; *C. v.* 'Purpurea Plena Elegans' – violet-purple double flowers. (makes unusual cut flowers); *C. v.* 'Royal Velours' – reddish-purple sepals and reddish stamens; *C. v.* 'Rubra' – velvety crimson sepals and brown stamens. 'Margot Koster' and 'Mme Julia Correvon', because of size of bloom, are described with the Large-Flowered Hybrids (see page 71). The viticellas, from southern Europe, are outstanding for their hardiness, free flowering and disease resistance. They comfortably head the table for the species in the International Clematis Society list.

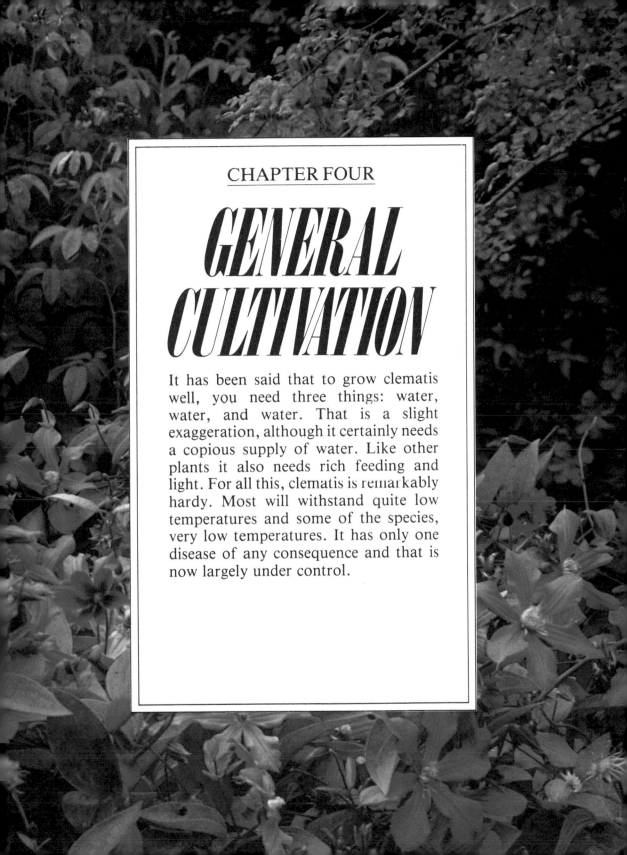

CHAPTER FOUR

GENERAL CULTIVATION

It has been said that to grow clematis well, you need three things: water, water, and water. That is a slight exaggeration, although it certainly needs a copious supply of water. Like other plants it also needs rich feeding and light. For all this, clematis is remarkably hardy. Most will withstand quite low temperatures and some of the species, very low temperatures. It has only one disease of any consequence and that is now largely under control.

The secret to growing healthy clematis is to pay particular attention to its care in the first two years. Its water supply can be effectively guarded by mulching in the summer – a neglected cultural aspect but one of great importance. So hardy is clematis that even if a plant appears to be dead, it may still reappear next year, or even the year after.

TOOLS FOR GROWING CLEMATIS

The following are required: a medium-sized spade, a medium-sized fork (both for digging holes; medium-sized tools are much less exhausting than large tools), a Dutch hoe (for hoeing with care; close work should be done by hand), secateurs and sharp scissors (both for pruning), a 5-litre (1-gallon) watering can, a rake, 5-litre (1-gallon) compression sprayer (for spraying fungicides and foliar feeding), a hosepipe (for watering), and a wheelbarrow. The following may prove useful: a kneeling pad, a 1 m (3 ft) ruler, durable labels, plastic ties (avoid the paper-covered ties), canes, and a number of different sized pots.

CHOOSING A PLANT

If you are ordering by post, then your order should go to the nursery in the spring for a plant which will be delivered in the autumn. This plant will be a small second-year plant (it was produced from a cutting taken in the previous spring). Immediately you receive the plant, dip it in a bucket of water for an hour. It should be kept until the spring or, ideally, the plant should now be repotted into a larger pot, given regular liquid fertilizer in the autumn (it will make a lot of growth), kept over the winter in a sheltered place (clematis are very hardy), and planted out when the soil is warm in the spring. Or, if you are a perfectionist, in the spring it can be repotted into an even larger pot, given regular liquid feeds to produce a large healthy plant, and kept in its pot for yet another year.

There is much to be said for visiting a specialist clematis nursery to collect your plant. There are now specialist nurseries in every part of the world and an international list can be obtained from the International Clematis Society. When you visit, especially in the summer, you can see the plants for yourself and at the same time glean valuable information from the nurseryman.

If you visit in the spring, the plants for sale will be second-year plants from cuttings taken in the previous spring. Unlike those picked up during late summer or autumn, these can be planted right away if strong plants, but some will prefer repotting into a larger pot, given regular feeding, and keeping for another year. You should always do this with plants picked up in the autumn.

When selecting a particular plant at a nursery, look for one or two good, healthy stems coming from the base. Inspect the stems to see if they have good, strong buds low down on the stem. These suggest a healthy plant. If you are fortunate, a new stem may be appearing through the soil.

There is a simple, effective way of repotting plants (see Fig. 9). First, fill a

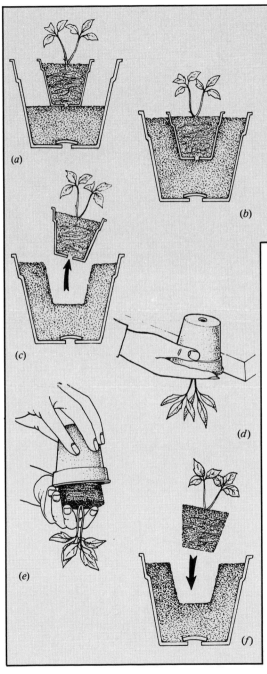

9. The easy way to repot plants.

(*a*) *Fill the larger pot with compost so that when the 'planted pot' is placed on the compost its rim is level with that of the larger pot.*

(*b*) *Add more compost firmly around the 'planted pot'.*

(*c*) *Take out the 'planted pot', leaving its imprint.*

(*d*) *Invert the 'planted pot' between the fingers of your right hand and tap against a bench.*

(*e*) *The plant will fall into your right hand.*

(*f*) *The plant will then fit the hole left in the larger pot.*

larger pot with some compost and then place the smaller pot (with the clematis) in the larger pot to see if the edge of the small pot is level with the edge of the larger pot. If not, you add more peat or compost at the bottom until the edge of the inner pot is level with the edge of the outer pot. Add compost all round the small pot, firming it gently down until the large pot is filled to the brim. You now take out the smaller pot from inside the larger pot. Holding the small pot with the clematis in the left hand, slip the base of the stems between the fingers of your right hand, invert the pot and cane, tap the pot edge gently on the edge of a bench or on the top of a fork stuck in the ground (or tap edge of pot with a stick) and immediately the clematis will slip out of its pot. The clematis will now fit perfectly into the space previously made in the larger pot. Gently firm and the job is done.

Pots can be earthenware, plastic or fibre. If your clematis is put into a fibre pot, then it makes planting so much easier. You do not need to take the

Alpinas are hardy, early flowering, and easy to grow. 'Frances Rivis', seen here, is most popular for its large, deep blue, nodding bells.

clematis out of the fibre pot but simply place the whole pot in the hole at its permanent location; the fibre will disintegrate. Should a clematis be in a flexible plastic container, then cut the container away before repotting the plant or placing it in the ground.

Clematis will do well in any good potting peat mixture. Soil-based composts are also satisfactory. Some of the experts make up their own mixture. One recommendation is a one-third clay, one-third sand, one-third loam mixture; the clay and sand come from deep deposits and are therefore likely to be sterile, reducing the risk of fungus. Others use 65% peat, together with grit and bark to aerate the peat.

THE PLANTING

Plan your planting some time beforehand. Indeed time can be devoted to it in the winter. It is said that an hour's gardening in winter is as good as five hours in the summer. Make a plan of your garden and decide where clematis can be planted with advantage. Chapter 2 contains plenty of ideas to inspire.

If you have good, rich, loamy soil, then planting is a simple matter. Just make a hole deep enough for your clematis and pop it in. Light soil, of course, will need humus, as will a heavy clay soil. In addition, a clay soil may need drainage at the bottom of a hole – either broken brick or rubble to a depth of 10–15 cm (4–6 in). Clematis will grow in either an acid or an alkaline soil, as long as neither is extreme in acidity or alkalinity. Leave the surface of the planting hole below the surface of the ground, to make a saucer about 2.5 cm (1 in) deep. This will assist watering. The species need the least preparation. Clematis should be planted at least 60 cm (24 in) apart.

Clematis are best planted in the spring. It is convenient for nurseries to deliver plants in the autumn, as understandably they don't wish to store them over the winter. But spring is a better time for planting as the soil is warmer and this is the time when a plant naturally wants to make growth. The evergreen clematis, as they are tender, should be planted in the late spring.

Care must be taken to plant clematis 45 cm–60 cm (18–24 in) away from walls. Soil close to walls tends to be dry and poor. Furthermore, walls absorb moisture, and there may even be an overhang which prevents rain reaching the clematis. The stems can be brought to the wall by cane, by wire or by string, the cane being the simplest. Should it be imperative to have a clematis planted right next to a wall, then this is possible, but in this event the preparation must be treated as if you are planting a clematis in a container, with special attention given to watering at all times. Even in the winter a plant in such a position can dry out and die if not given special attention.

Earlier it was said that if you have good soil, planting clematis is easy. But what if your soil is poor, and it can be poor in a number of ways? What is a five-minute job on good soil becomes a thirty-minute job on poor soil; but the end result will be worth it. The instructions given below lean towards perfection; they can be modified slightly if there is a real lack of time or strength.

When digging a hole, mark out the area on the soil surface. There should be a 45 cm (18 in) diameter and the hole should be 60 cm (24 in) deep. (This depth means you will remove nearly a barrowload of soil.) Having removed the top layer with the spade, loosen the next layer with the fork before using the spade again to lift the soil out. Keep on loosening the soil with the fork and this will make your task much easier. Any soil that you discard should be put in the wheelbarrow and taken away. (Keep good top soil.) The commonest error is not to make the hole deep enough so that it is impossible to plant the clematis at a good depth with 10 cm (4 in) of soil covering it. However, strength can give out.

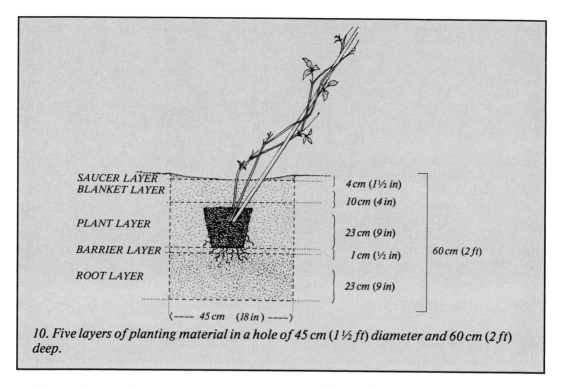

10. Five layers of planting material in a hole of 45 cm (1½ ft) diameter and 60 cm (2 ft) deep.

When planting, it is convenient to think of five layers in the hole (see Fig. 10). The first, bottom layer is where the roots will be growing. It is known that clematis roots extend for at least 45–60 cm (18–24 in). Thus 23 cm (9 in) of planting material is given to this layer, to give roots a good start. The roots need a rich medium for nourishment and also a medium which will retain water. Experts vary in their recommendations. A common recommendation is half soil with half manure, or moist, coarse, peat or with leaf mould. Another recommendation is for half soil and half garden compost. Whatever is employed, in addition there should be added two handfuls (200 g/7 oz) of bonemeal, and this should be well mixed in. The second layer should be a mere 1 cm (½ in) of soil or peat, and is simply a barrier to keep the roots of the new plant initially separate from the rich material below. The third layer of 23 cm (9 in) is where the clematis will be placed. The fourth layer is above the clematis and extends to 10 cm (4 in) as a blanket to the plant; thus the stock of the plant will have 10 cm (4 in) blanket of material above it. The material in the third and fourth layers need not be as rich

Opposite: C. armandii *is an early-flowering, tall-growing clematis with handsome evergreen leathery foliage. It produces a profusion of white or creamy fragrant flowers. Ideal for a sheltered wall.*

as the material in the bottom area and can consist of good top soil taken out of the hole, or soil mixed with peat or leaf mould, or compost. One handful of bone-meal (100 g/3½ oz) should be added and mixed well into the third and fourth layer material. The fifth layer is the lip area, allowing 4 cm (1½ in) below the soil level to make a saucer area into which water can collect, either naturally or as a result of watering. Thus, avoid leaving the soil convex at the top; this saucer area will greatly facilitate the task of watering.

First put the chosen material in the root layer. Cover with a thin layer of soil or peat to make the barrier layer. Before planting the clematis make sure that it is moist by soaking it in a bucket of water for two hours. Extract the plant from the pot by knocking on the edge of a shelf or a fork, as described earlier. In the case of the large-bloomed hybrids, gently spread the lace like roots over the surface of the barrier area. In the case of species clematis, on no account touch the thread-like roots. Now fill in with the material chosen for the plant layer and the blanket layer. Leave a saucer layer at the top. Firm the material around and above the plant with your foot. Supply shade, as discussed later, by mulching. If a cane is not used, then mark the planting area with a short cane or stick which will prevent the clematis, once planted, from getting lost. Clematis plants which are planted together should be at least 60 cm (24 in) apart.

Some gardeners with poor soil will just not have the strength and time for the above thorough method. They can modify the above plan or use a quick way

of planting clematis which gives good results. This is as follows. In the bottom of a hole place the contents of one tomato growbag, strengthened with bonemeal and a general fertilizer. Plant the clematis in its fibre pot in the top half, and place the material from another growbag around it. Keep watering as fibre pots can dry out very quickly.

The stems of the clematis plant arrive from the nursery attached to a cane. Make sure the stems are firmly attached to the cane and, if need be, use new ties. This cane helps to support the stem during planting. Once the plant is safely in the hole this cane, if long enough, can carry

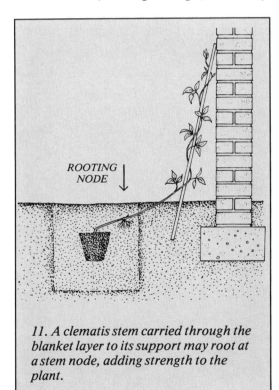

ROOTING NODE

11. A clematis stem carried through the blanket layer to its support may root at a stem node, adding strength to the plant.

the stem to a wall, post, host plant, or other climbing support. If the cane is too short then, after planting the clematis, use a new cane of the desired length, insert this near the original cane, and gently tie the old cane to the new. The stem will happily climb from the old cane to the new and onwards to the wall, post, host plant, or other climbing support. A variant on the above is to detach the stem from the cane after planting the clematis in the planting layer, and lead the stem through the blanket area to a cane near the wall, post, host plant, or other

support. There is usually a node in the stem which will root, giving added strength to the plant (see Fig. 11).

During planting, advantage can be taken to insert a watering tube into the soil. The aim is to lead the water straight to the rich root area. A pipe of 12 cm (4½ in) diameter and 38 cm (15 in) long will do the job. At the bottom end of the tube there should be a few stones, to allow easy drainage. An alternative watering aid is currently to sink an empty plant pot close to the clematis stem and water through this (see Fig. 12).

A plant which needs to be moved from one part of the garden to another should be dug up in the late autumn/winter or early spring and moved to the new location. If the soil is poor, it should be given the thorough treatment mentioned earlier (see page 92). When moving a plant, it is better to remove most of the top growth to give it a better chance. Try not to cut into the old, woody, stems which have no buds on them; you need to retain some of the non-woody stems. The species do not move as well as the large-flowered cultivars.

If you want to have exceptional clematis plants, there is much to be said for keeping plants in pots for another year after arrival from a nursery, so that they are really strong when planted in the ground. If a plant is being kept in a pot for a fourth year, then repot at the start of the year to a larger pot and fertilize with liquid manure at regular intervals.

Planting in a hole in a patio or under concrete allows clematis to do very well as, of course, the plant is provided with permanent mulch.

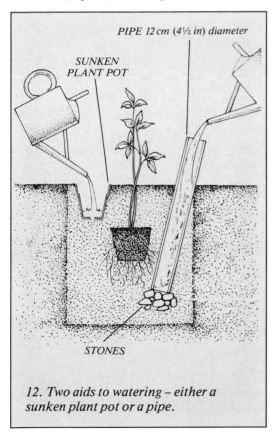

PIPE 12 cm (4½ in) diameter

SUNKEN PLANT POT

STONES

12. Two aids to watering – either a sunken plant pot or a pipe.

PLANTING CLEMATIS IN A CONTAINER

A container should be at least 46 cm (18 in) deep and 30 cm (12 in) in diameter. In such a small pot, there should be drainage material for 2–3 cm ($\frac{3}{4}$–$1\frac{1}{4}$ in), plus an insecticide sprayed in it. In larger pots this layer will be deeper. The container should be off the ground and contain drainage holes in its base. It can be filled with soil-based composts or soil and manure with bonemeal, or garden compost and bonemeal. The clematis should, if possible, be planted deep in the container, around 10 cm (4 in) below the soil level. A 3 cm (1 in) lip should be left at the top of the container to make a saucer for watering. Each spring, one or more hand-fuls of sulphate of potash (depending on the size of the container) should be worked into the planting material. This should be repeated in mid-summer. The early large-flowered hybrids should be pruned harder than usual in their first season, to produce a healthy plant. The stems should be trained around the supports which spring from the pot. Tie the stems as horizontally as possible but allowing light to get in. Ideally, the top 8–10 cm (3–4 in) of the planting material should be replaced every spring; in small pots most of the material may need changing every year.

Plants that perform well in containers include 'Niobe', Jackmanii types, viticella types, and the early large-flowered hybrids. Pots of bulbs, geraniums, etc. can be placed on top of the soil of the container, although these should never be planted in the soil itself. The growth of the clematis can be retarded by putting it in the shade. Then it can be moved into the sun or under glass when flowering is required. If unusually hot, the container can be kept moist by putting it inside another container with moist peat between the two.

LABELLING

Put the name of the clematis on a label and tie it to a support close to that plant. Don't tie it to the plant; they don't like it and the label is likely to disappear with the first pruning. Check your labels every year. Keep a plan of your garden, on which the position of each clematis is noted; orientate yourself by relating the position of a clematis to a permanent feature nearby, for example a rose, a mark on the wall, a nearby shrub, etc.

FIRST TWO YEARS

Care during this period, more than at any other time, guarantees the growth of a fine plant. The gardener should concentrate less on producing bloom than on producing a healthy plant. Attention is required in the following areas:

☐ PRUNING

In the case of the large-flowered cultivars, wait for one month so that the plant can be fully established in the ground. Then inspect the stem, looking for two good buds about 30 cm (12 in) from the ground. Pinch out the stems above the buds (see Fig. 13), to reduce the amount of foliage and so reduce the strain on the roots; it will also encourage new shoots to appear.

As the new shoots make growths of about 30 cm (12 in) then pinch out again above the buds, and by continuing to do this, you will end up with a nicely branched plant (see Fig. 13). Should you be so fortunate as to have two stems coming from the base, then the same treatment is given to both stems, with one stem veered to the left and the other stem veered to the right. The species plants do not require this treatment.

□ WATERING

Each plant must receive at least 10 litres (2 gallons) of water per week.

□ FERTILIZING

Rich fertilizing is not required during the first year as the plant has already been given sufficient nutriment in the soil.

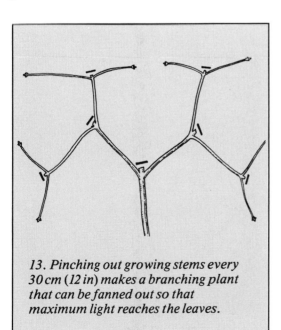

13. Pinching out growing stems every 30 cm (12 in) makes a branching plant that can be fanned out so that maximum light reaches the leaves.

However, liquid fertilizer should be applied once a week during the growing period. During the second year and thereafter, the plant should be fertilized according to instructions given later (see page 100).

□ WILT CONTROL

Clematis plants are most susceptible to wilt during the first two years; when woody stems develop, the risk becomes much less. Carefully observe the instructions given later (see page 106).

SUPPORT

Being a clinging vine, all clematis require supports to cling to. This they arrange for themselves by using petioles to attach on to something, whether this is wire or other artificial support, or a host plant. Types of support have already been discussed (Chapter 2). A clematis can grow 60 cm (24 in) in a week, so there is a need to train once a week during the growing season, gently guiding the stem where you want it to go. Frequently the clematis stem may need to be tied to the artificial support or to the host plant so that it stays put. This can be done by using plastic covered ties; paper covered ties should be avoided as they deteriorate so quickly. The tie should not be too tight, as it may obstruct further growth or even crush the stem. At first, errors will be made, but you will soon become adept at tying up clematis successfully. Herbaceous clematis do not require tying usually, but they may need some support in the form of short poles or branches to clamber over.

Opposite: *Some clematis rely on large blooms for effect. Some rely for mass effect on myriad small flowers;* C. flammula *is one of these. It also gives off overpowering scent in the autumn.*

How can you provide support to container-grown clematis, which can so easily be knocked over by wind? These potted clematis may be awaiting planting, or are being moved between a nursery area and a conservatory. If two strong poles are placed at a distance from one another, a wire can be strung between them. The canes of the individual clematis pots can then be tied to this wire and they will survive any amount of buffeting from wind (see Fig. 14).

FEEDING

In a good loamy soil, little or no fertilizing will be necessary. Copious watering, however, is always required. Some soils will need feeding.

Manure and garden compost have low amounts of nutrients but they give invaluable humus to the soil, improving drainage and the retention of water. Thus most energy must be given to the plants in the form of fertilizers. These should be spread evenly and uniformly around the plant and worked gently into the soil either by hand or fork or hoe. Manure and garden compost should be kept away from the base of the stems, at least to a distance of 10 cm (4 in). Even more important is to make sure that artificial fertilizers are spread well away from the stems of the plant; most of the roots are

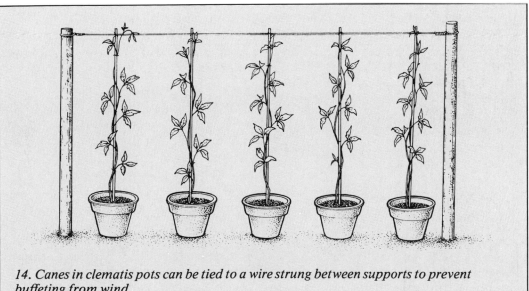

14. *Canes in clematis pots can be tied to a wire strung between supports to prevent buffeting from wind.*

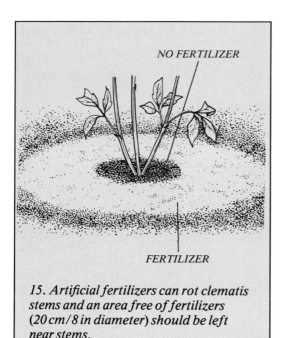

NO FERTILIZER

FERTILIZER

15. Artificial fertilizers can rot clematis stems and an area free of fertilizers (20 cm/8 in diameter) should be left near stems.

spread widely below the plant and the fertilizer will reach them better away from the stem base (see Fig. 15). Another important reason is that artificial fertilizer can rot the stems and even kill a plant. Peat, although it contains no nourishment, is a good mulch and a soil conditioner; if used, it should be strengthened by containing an artificial fertilizer.

□ FEEDING SCHEDULE

IN THE AUTUMN
1. Apply bonemeal at the rate of 100 g (3½ oz) per sq m (sq yd). Bonemeal is a slow-release fertilizer and will be still at work in the following spring and longer. It tends to make the ground alkaline. It is rich in phosphates and encourages root growth. It should be worked gently into the soil.
2. Provide a mulch of garden compost or well rotted manure, spreading it to about 60 cm (2 ft) around the plant; it must be well rotted manure and should cut like a cake.

IN THE SPRING
1. Gently dig in the autumn manure.
2. Apply a handful of potash or an artificial fertilizer rich in potash. Water it into the soil.
3. Now apply a mulch of suitable material or manure.
4. Apply a liquid fertilizer rich in potash, once a week if possible. A well established plant will even benefit from a liquid feed twice a week. Never apply the fertilizer stronger than stated in the instructions; 'Little and often' is the secret to success. Water first if the soil is dry. Stop the liquid manure when the clematis is in flower, as it will shorten the flowering period. Continue thereafter right into the autumn.

IN MID-SUMMER
1. Apply another handful of potash or a fertilizer rich in potash. Water it in. This will help the second flowering of the clematis.
2. Continue the liquid feeding as above.

FOLIAR FEEDING

This can be an additional valuable aid to the plant. With a compression sprayer, and using a fine spray, spray both sides of the leaves. Follow the instructions of the supplier. Give half strength until the plant is established. Thereafter it can be full strength or even double strength. Never spray in the sun as leaves can be scorched.

WATERING

The importance of giving clematis a sufficient amount of water cannot be overestimated; after watering, you can almost see the plant growing. In theory it is possible to overwater; a hose directed continually at a piece of ground would ultimately leech all the nutrients out of it. In the amounts recommended for a clematis, this is unlikely to happen and in any event is counterbalanced by the rich feeding programme.

A clematis plant requires a minimum of 5 litres (1 gallon) of water a week. But it will profit from as much as 20 litres (4 gallons) per plant per week if possible. During very hot weather it may require 5 litres (1 gallon) per plant per day. It is best to 'point' water, i.e. to direct the water specifically on to the clematis plant rather than assume it will take its share from a more general garden watering; in this way you can determine exactly how much water you are giving. Watering should take place out of the sun in the evenings. If a hose is used, then use a fine spray on both sides of the leaves. If a pipe is being used alongside the plant, then put two-thirds of the water into the pipe and the rest over the soil to keep moist any roots which are near the surface. If a liquid fertilizer is being used at the same time, this can be placed in a watering can and the water added from the hose so that the fertilizer is dissolved and diluted; the water with the diluted fertilizer is applied from the can. Watering will, of course, be assisted by having planted your clematis correctly with a saucer area at the top of the hole (see page 92).

MULCHING

The main reason for using a mulch with clematis is to retain the moisture in the ground. This is much more effective than planting the roots in the shade, or planting shrubs around it. Additional reasons for using a mulch are that it keeps the ground cool, it suppresses weeds, it adds humus to the ground and it will also help to add nutrients to the soil. If sterilized mulch material is used, for example peat or sterilized mushroom compost, then it may help to protect the plant against wilt as it will not contain spores of the fungus.

Before applying the mulch, remove any dead material on the ground and burn it. Add any fertilizers that are required and, if the ground is dry, water it. Apply sufficient mulch material to cover 60 sq cm (2 sq ft) around the plant, and to a thickness of at least 5–8 cm (2–3 in) – 8–10 cm (3–4 in) would be better (see Fig. 16). Do not carry the mulch material close to the stems. In the autumn the material can be forked gently into the ground or left to protect the roots against a severe climate.

The following materials can be used:

1. Mushroom compost. This is often sterilized. It is alkaline and therefore particularly good for acid soils. Excellent mulching material. Not to be used if

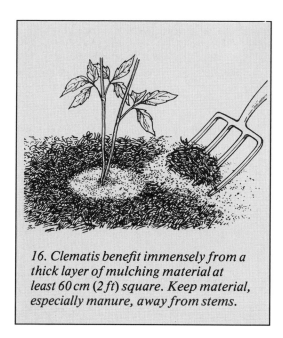

16. Clematis benefit immensely from a thick layer of mulching material at least 60 cm (2 ft) square. Keep material, especially manure, away from stems.

acidity needs to be retained for other plants.

2. Moist peat. This contains a little nitrogen only. It tends towards acidity and is therefore good for alkaline soils.

3. Leaf mould. Contains some nutrients. It is usually acid. Excellent mulching material.

4. Farmyard manure. Tends to be acid.

5. Garden compost. Tends to be acid.

6. Well rotted straw or sawdust.

7. Grass clippings. Tends to take the nitrogen out of the soil. Not recommended if a selected weed killer has been used on the lawn.

8. Pulverized bark. Contains little nutrients.

9. Black polythene sheeting, or porous sheeting, with a hole in the sheeting from which the clematis emerges. Can be disguised with bark or stones.

10. As a last resort, stones, small bricks, grit or shingle can also be used.

If you use materials which are liable to take nitrogen out of the soil, then 60–90 g (2–3 oz) of sulphate of ammonia can be spread over the ground to the sq m (sq yd) before applying the mulch. The mulch should be applied in the spring after the soil has warmed up. Later, inorganic fertilizers or liquid fertilizers can be applied through it. Recently there has appeared on the market a porous sheeting which prevents weeds coming through, retains water in the soil and at the same time, being porous, allows water and fertilizers to pass easily through.

Plants can, of course, create shade but they also tend to take water and nutrients out of the ground. The most suitable plants to use for shading are primulas, pansies, dwarf lavenders and the small potentillas.

PRUNING

This is easy if the following principles are understood:

1. You must remember the classification of the clematis into two groups. In Group I there are the early species (*a*) and early large-flowered hybrids (*b*). In Group II there are the late-flowering species (*a*), the late large-flowered hybrids (*b*), and herbaceous clematis.

2. The early-flowering clematis (Group I) require little pruning. The late-flowering clematis (Group II) need much pruning.

3. What is the explanation for the different pruning methods in (2) above?

The early clematis will flower on growth made the previous year. Therefore it makes sense to prune lightly in the spring or one will destroy the growth which has been produced and on which we get the flowers. Late-flowering clematis, on the other hand, flower late in the season and on the growth made the same year. Therefore it makes sense to prune hard early in the season, to produce good growth which will make for an abundance of bloom later on.

4. If in any doubt consult the list in this book about which pruning method to adopt (see Chapter 2), or any catalogue from your local nursery.

5. If you make an error, *nil desperandum* (don't despair!). If you pruned the early clematis hard, then they will simply flower later. If you give little pruning to the late-flowering clematis, it simply means that they will be perhaps less productive than they might have been, and will be rather straggly at the base. If you forget to prune entirely you should still find a reasonable display of blooms.

☐ HOW TO PRUNE

Group I (*a*). Early species – TIDY.
In late spring/early summer, after flowering, cut the shoots to tidy the plant so that it fits comfortably the space you are giving it. It will have plenty of time to grow and make good shoots for flowering next year.

Group I (*b*). Early large-flowered hybrids – LIGHT pruning.
In late winter/early spring trim out the dead growth and leaf growth. Then lightly trim the shoots back to the first pair of strong buds high up on the shoot. As the buds are high up you should not be taking much away. If, on the other hand, you have a tangled mass at the top, prune just below it. Fan the remainder out.

Group II (*a*) and (*b*). Late-flowering species and late-flowering large-flowered hybrids – HARD pruning.
In late winter/early spring cut above a good pair of buds near the ground. It may be as low as 8–30 cm (3 in–12 in) from the ground. If you happen to cut to the ground, don't worry as new shoots will appear from the soil.

☐ ADDITIONAL POINTS

The above are all the simple instructions you need for general pruning. However, with time you may like to experiment with some more advanced variations of pruning. Here are some suggestions.

1. If your Group I (*b*) (large-flowered hybrids) become rather a tangled mass after a few years, cut them down after flowering below the tangle, even if you are down to a short distance from the ground, but don't cut into thick, woody, stems. Your clematis will make good growth by the end of the year and produce good blooms the next season.

2. If you don't want Group I (*b*) (large-flowered hybrids) to flower early, prune them hard in late winter/early spring and they will give you the blooms in summer instead of spring.

3. If you want Group I (*b*) (large-flowered hybrids) to flower early *and* late, then hard prune some stems in late winter/early spring and they will flower

Opposite:
C. florida *'Sieboldiana', a Japanese clematis.*
This delicate clematis is eye catching due to
the dramatic contrast between its greenish-
white tepals and prominent purple stamens.

late, and leave the rest to flower early. You
can reverse the process the following year.
4 If you have the time and you want to
make sure Group I(*b*) (large-flowered
hybrids) will produce a good show the
following year, for example in a
container, then after flowering trim again
to good buds on each shoot.
5. If you want Group II(*b*) (late
large-flowering hybrids) to flower early
then *don't* prune in late winter/early
spring.
6. When you prune Group II (*b*) (late
large-flowering hybrids) in late
winter/early spring, prune the shoots at
different lengths. Long ones will flower
early and the short ones late.
7. If Group II (*b*) (late large-flowered
hybrids) look a mess in the autumn,
perhaps on the heather bed, hard prune
them back then; they will come to no
harm. If in a tree, undo the ties, tug, and it
will all come away. You can hard prune
then, or coil up the stems and prune in the
spring as usual.
8. With young plants you can remove the
seed heads as they are produced so that all
the energy goes into the growth. This is
not necessary with established plants.
9. If you don't know which group a plant
belongs to, let it grow a year and it will
become apparent.

By now you will have broken all the rules!

☐ EXTRA POINTS ON PRUNING

1. Use secateurs or scissors, depending on
the toughness of the shoots.
2. Always burn shoots at once after
pruning. This will reduce the risk of
leaving spores of wilt around.
3. *Never cut into strong woody stems.*
Clematis don't like it and the plant is
liable to give up the ghost.

DISEASES AND PESTS

These are not many and will be taken in
order of importance.

☐ CLEMATIS WILT

The cause for this is now known, and it is
due to a fungus.

In the last century wilt was unknown.
However, as a result of the cross breeding
at that time, the vulnerability to wilt
developed in clematis with the result that
by the early part of this century
nurserymen lost interest in the plant. It
was W. O. Gloyer in the United States in
1915 who isolated the fungus responsible –
Ascochyta clematidina (Thümen). His
work was confirmed by two researchers,
Ebben and Last, in the UK in 1965. The
work of some Dutch researchers has also
suggested that there may be one, or
possibly two, other fungi involved. The
spores of the fungus are present in soil and
on plants. When the right temperature
and humidity is reached the fungus
becomes active and strikes the clematis in
a characteristic fashion: it works itself
around the stem of the clematis,
ultimately cutting off the flow of sap up
the stem. The stem dies. It usually attacks
one stem but it may attack several. It may

attack a stem high up but most commonly it attacks at, or about, soil level. Predispositions to attack are injury of the plant, which allows the spore to enter or too strong growth of the stem which may weaken the plant. The unfortunate gardener goes to bed admiring a healthy green plant and wakes up in the morning only to find that the stem or stems are hanging limply. Attacks are much more common in the first two years; when the clematis develops a woody stem it seems that the fungus is unable to penetrate. The species, especially the early-blooming species, are less likely to be attacked.

Wilt can be prevented as follows:

1. During the first two years it is important to pinch back the clematis continually, encouraging side shoots and, by reducing the foliage, reducing the strain on the roots.
2. All prunings, twigs, and dead material around the clematis should be collected and burnt. There may be fungal spores in this material.
3. A mulch of sterile material such as peat or mushroom compost around the base of the plant will help, as it acts as a barrier to any spores in the ground.
4. If healthy growth has been encouraged in the first two years more than one stem may appear above the surface. If one stem is attacked, then the others may be spared and thus there is little effect on the plant.
5. The clematis should be deeply planted. In that way, if a shoot is killed to ground level, a new shoot will appear from a node below the soil surface.
6. Regular spraying helps. Systemic fungicides are the best. The instructions on the preparation should be followed for strength. Do not spray in the sun or on a windy day. Spray both sides of the leaves. Soak the ground as well as the plant. Spray every two to three weeks in the early season and then once a month. Next season change the preparation employed. After three years the spraying becomes less important. To help keep it efficient, always wash out the equipment after use. Preparations which can be employed include benomyl, Bordeaux Mixture, carbendazim, and propiconazole.

If, despite the above, your clematis is stricken, then there is only one thing to do. Cut the damaged stem right down to a healthy node on the stem and, if necessary, right down to ground level. Burn the cut material. Continue to treat the plant as if it were untouched, paying particular attention to watering. A new shoot or shoots will appear from the ground and, given good fortune, they will remain healthy. It has been known for stems of the same plant to be struck two or three times but ultimately to produce a healthy plant.

☐ MILDEW

While wilt tends to appear in the early season, powdery mildew (which shows as a white, powdery deposit on leaves and shoot tips) will tend to appear during the mid-season. It disfigures flowers, leaves and young stems. It succumbs very well to fungicides.

☐ PESTS

Earwigs may produce holes in the leaves. They can be treated by pyrethrum or gamma-HCH. Earwigs can be captured in inverted pots on canes, with straw inside.

Slugs will tend to eat new shoots. Ashes of wood or coke or coal can be spread around the plant to deter them. Slug bait can be employed. Garlic or sage can be planted alongside. A beer trap can be arranged by placing a can of beer level with the soil. The slugs drop in, get drunk, and drown!

Aphids succumb to the above insecticides. The red spider can be a nuisance in greenhouses but is killed by pirimiphos-methyl.

Vine weevil can cause a plant to die in the pot. Search for the weevil inside the pot. Water with an insecticide containing gamma-HCH.

ROUND-THE-YEAR CARE

EARLY WINTER
- plan clematis planting for next year; order plants.

MID-WINTER
- dig holes for new clematis; order tools, fungicides, peat, manure, fertilizers, etc; water any plants liable to dry out.

LATE WINTER
- move and split up established plants; water plants liable to dry out.

EARLY SPRING
- lightly trim early large-flowered hybrids; prune hard late-flowering large-flowered hybrids and species; fan out the pruned clematis and give support as required; apply sulphate of potash (a handful for each plant) away from the stock, and water in.

MID-SPRING
- start spraying fungicide programme; plant new clematis and prune hard; start liquid fertilizer programme; start watering programme.

LATE SPRING
- prune early species after flowering; apply mulches; take cuttings; layer plants; continue watering programme.

EARLY SUMMER
- prune early large-flowered hybrids after flowering if they require it, especially those in containers; keep up watering, liquid feeding and fungicide programmes; cut flowers for the house.

MID-SUMMER
- second feeding of sulphate of potash (a handful for each plant) and water in; keep up watering, liquid feeding and fungicide programmes; cut blooms for the house.

LATE SUMMER
-keep up watering, liquid feeding and fungicide programmes; cut blooms for the house; check supports for late-flowering species.

EARLY AUTUMN
- gather seed and sow the seed; layer late-flowering hybrids and species.

MID-AUTUMN
- collect seed heads for decoration or drying; reduce watering; stop liquid fertilizer and fungicide programmes.

LATE AUTUMN
- in very cold areas, check protection of plants. Water plants liable to dry out.

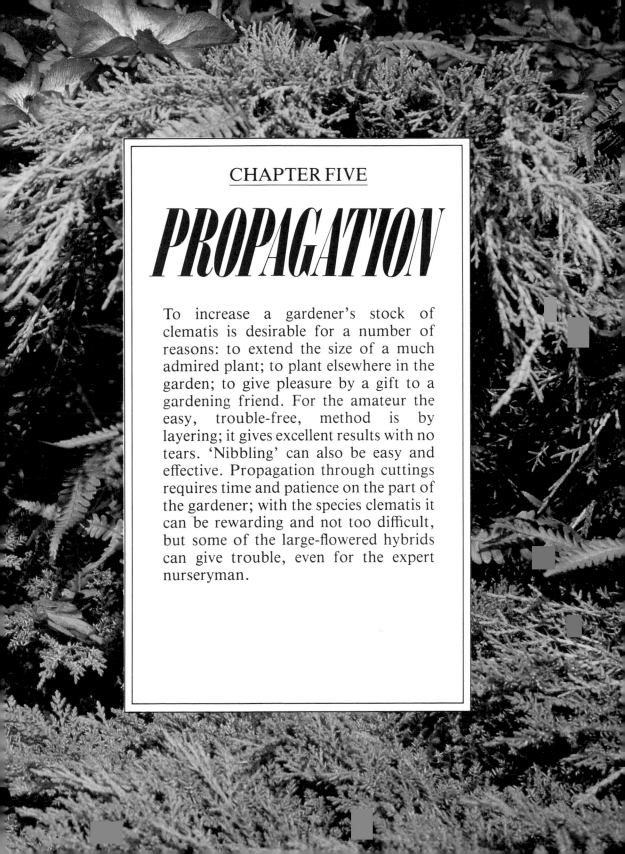

CHAPTER FIVE

PROPAGATION

To increase a gardener's stock of clematis is desirable for a number of reasons: to extend the size of a much admired plant; to plant elsewhere in the garden; to give pleasure by a gift to a gardening friend. For the amateur the easy, trouble-free, method is by layering; it gives excellent results with no tears. 'Nibbling' can also be easy and effective. Propagation through cuttings requires time and patience on the part of the gardener; with the species clematis it can be rewarding and not too difficult, but some of the large-flowered hybrids can give trouble, even for the expert nurseryman.

Layering

This is the best propagation procedure when a small number of plants are required. The main advantage, of course, is that they come true to type; the offspring will have the identical characteristics of the parent. Another advantage is that the method can be used to extend an existing plant on one or both sides. The extended plant makes a larger impact. Furthermore, should the original plant die there will be replacement plants.

Layering can begin as soon as the ground gets warm in the early spring. It can be used with the species and also with the large-flowered hybrids. In the case of the late large-flowered hybrids, some stems can be left unpruned during the spring pruning and these can be used for layering. These spring-layered plants will have formed roots by the autumn and will be ready for potting up. Layering can, of course, occur at any time until the autumn; but in this event the plants may not be ready in the autumn and thus need to stay in the ground until they are ready some time the following year.

Many of the strong-growing clematis do not require elaborate procedures. Simply bring the stem down to the ground, make a trench 10–15 cm (4–6 in) deep with your hand or trowel, gently lay the stem in the trench, pull the soil over it, place a brick over the node, and fix the end of the stem to a cane. Using a simple method like this probably means that you will attempt to layer many more clematis.

C. fusca has unusual, arresting, unclematis-like flowers. Four thick tepals make an urn-shaped flower. The tepals, though purple, are covered with dark brown hairs on the outside, giving a dark colour that contrasts with the pale green interior of the urn. A lovely cut flower.

17. Layering clematis

(a) *Layer is held in soil by bent wire; cut-through node is held open with a matchstick; and stem is supported with a cane.*

(b) *Layering as* (a) *but into a pot*

(c) *Serpentine layering either into soil or a series of pots*

A more exacting method is as follows:
1. A long stem is gently brought down towards the ground. Old material and not green material is best for layering.
2. Carefully inspect the stem to see where there are good nodes. With a sharp knife, cut below the node joint, slicing upwards about half way through the joint to make a short 'tongue'. To keep the 'tongue' open, slip a match or pebble in the elbow (see Fig. 17).
3. Powder the joint with hormone rooting powder.
4. With a trowel, make a trench 10–15 cm (4–6 in) deep. In the trench place peat and soil, or potting compost and soil or sharp sand. Gently peg the node down into this mixture using a piece of wire bent to the shape of a hairpin. Cover the node with the mixture.
5. Cover the node with a good mulch, or stones, or a brick, to keep the area moist.
6. Mark the end of the stem with a short cane, which will remind you where the layer is, and fix the stem (see Fig. 17).
7. Water freely and keep watered.
8. Instead of putting the node in the trench as indicated, the node can be gently laid into a mixture in a 25 cm (10 in) pot. The mixture can be soil-based potting compost, or peat and soil, or compost and soil (see Fig. 17).
9. Leave for 6–12 months. To test whether you have roots, gently pull on the end of the stem; if there is resistance you have roots.
10. With secateurs, sever the layered plant from the parent plant, gently lift with a fork and pot up immediately. Don't let the roots dry out. Water the pot. Give it liquid fertilizer feeds. When the

plant is strong, it can be planted out. In the method described under no. 8 above, the plant will be growing in a pot and, once severed from the parent plant, will need further time in the pot to become a strong plant.

Serpentine layering involves taking a particularly long shoot with a number of nodes. Each of the nodes is treated as above. The parts of the stem between nodes is above ground. The nodes can be in the ground or in pots in the ground (as no. 8 above). (See Fig. 17.)

TAKING CUTTINGS

Species clematis will do best by this method. Some vigorous large-flowered hybrids will also do well. The new plants will, of course, be true to type, in that they will have the same characteristics as the parents. Proceed as follows:

1. The sooner the cuttings are taken in the spring, the longer time they will have to become good, strong plants before the autumn. Check your plants to see if stems have been produced which will be suitable from which to take cuttings. The cuttings must be taken from stems which are firm and semi-hard. This usually means that the tip of the stem will produce cuttings which are too soft, and the bottom part of the stem will produce cuttings which are too hard. Thus the middle stem may be the most suitable. The ideal cutting is firm enough to slip into the cutting mixture with a firm push.

2. The potting mixture for the cutting should be 50% moss peat and 50% grit; others advocate two parts sharp sand and one part peat; still others use soil-based cuttings compost. The mixture should be sterilized.

3. An inter-nodal cutting is taken (find a node with its leaves, then cut between this node and the node below). Thus there is only a node at the top end of the cutting (see Fig. 18 *a* & *c*). The total length of the cutting should be between 2.5–5 cm (1–2 in). Should you come across a clematis with its nodes very close together, then you may need to use a nodal cutting. There will be a node at the top end and the bottom end of the cutting (see Fig. 18 *b* & *d*).

4. Spread the clematis stem on a bench and cut the cuttings with a sharp knife or razor blade. Keep the cuttings moist and use at once.

5. Trim off completely one set of the pair of leaves. The leaf that remains can also have its central leaflet cut off.

6. Quickly dip the cutting in water and then into hormone rooting powder, allowing a dip of about 2.5 cm (1 in) of the stem.

7. Gently but firmly push the cutting into the compost of a pot. Don't let the cuttings touch one another. The bud should be just resting on the surface of the mixture. The cuttings should be 8 cm (3 in) apart. The leaves should not touch other leaves, the compost or the pot's cover. Label the pot.

8. Spray the pot with water containing fungicide, such as benomyl or Bordeaux Mixture. Let the pot drain. The type of fungicide used should be changed every ten days.

9. Put the pot into either a propagator or a cold frame, or a pot covered with polythene; in the latter event, place four stakes at the circumference of the pot, to

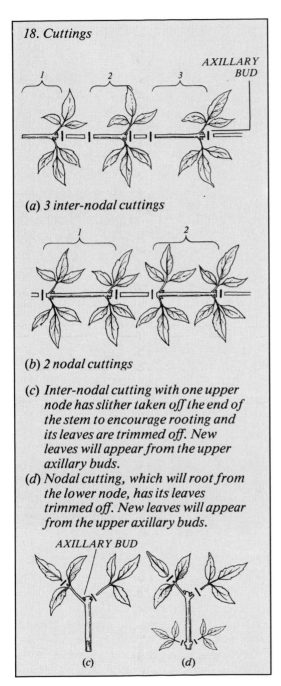

18. Cuttings

AXILLARY BUD

(a) 3 inter-nodal cuttings

(b) 2 nodal cuttings

(c) Inter-nodal cutting with one upper node has slither taken off the end of the stem to encourage rooting and its leaves are trimmed off. New leaves will appear from the upper axillary buds.

(d) Nodal cutting, which will root from the lower node, has its leaves trimmed off. New leaves will appear from the upper axillary buds.

AXILLARY BUD

(c)   (d)

keep the polythene away from the leaves (see Fig. 19). The plants must be kept in the shade. If bottom heating is available, it can be helpful in producing rooting; the temperature should be 23°C (73°F). Continue spraying with fungicide once a week: the container is taken out of its cover, sprayed, allowed to drain, and then put back under its cover.

10. The cuttings will root in about four to five weeks. It is usually obvious which have rooted. Tug gently on the cutting and if there is resistance, then roots have formed. A little air can now be allowed to

19. A polythene cover is supported by canes to keep it away from the leaves of cuttings in the pot.

The late-flowering C. orientalis *is popular for its yellow blooms followed by prominent seed heads. The largest flower is that of the variety 'Bill Mackenzie', shown here. The attractive foliage is finely cut.*

the plants and this can be increased each day until, in a few days, the cover is off. 11. After a further two to three weeks, plant out into 10 cm (4 in) pots, using a suitable potting mixture. Pinch or nip out any central growth, to encourage side shoots. Cover for a few days, after which allow air for one to two hours a day and then, after a few more days, the cover can be removed. Continue to spray with fungicide every week.

12. If good growth is made, the plants can be planted in the next largest pot. Again, pinch out central growth to encourage side growth. Keep spraying with fungicide once a week. Give liquid fertilizer once a week. The plants can be planted out in the following spring or can be kept for a further year in a pot. By now, you are admiring the hard work of a nurseryman!

Hardwood cuttings can be taken in late winter. This is applicable especially to *C. montana*, *C. chrysocoma*, *C.* × *jouiniana* and *C. heracleifolia*. The end of the internodal cutting should be bruised or wounded by taking a slither off. The cutting should be about 10 cm (4 in) long. They should be treated as above but no heating is required. The cuttings should always be in shade, kept moist and sprayed regularly with fungicides. They can be potted up in early summer into 10 cm (4 in) pots. They may be ready to be planted out into permanent quarters in the autumn, or kept another year in a larger pot.

Some of the species cuttings will root so easily that a number can be put together into water in a small vase, kept in a north-facing window, and the water changed regularly when it gets putrid. In a few weeks, with luck, roots will appear. These can then be potted up.

SEEDS

The achene (fruit) of the clematis consists of the base containing the seed and a tail of silky hairs which help to disperse the seed. Of the species, only the seed of some will produce worthwhile seedlings. The new plants will resemble the parent plant but may be poorer; a few may be better. Select the seed from good plants. The seed from the hybrid clematis will not resemble the parent at all. Thus it is a gamble germinating them, and a very large number are likely to be worthless. Occasionally a worthwhile plant will ensue. Very rarely a plant may be commercially viable.

The seed from the early clematis may be ready by mid-summer and can be used then. The seed of the late-flowering clematis are best kept until the following spring. If they are stored they should be kept in a polythene bag, labelled and put into a refrigerator, where they can be chilled to below 5°C (40°F) but not frozen.

The seeds should germinate on a seed medium in seed pans. Prick out as soon as the seeds can be handled and put into soil-based seed compost. The seeds of the species will usually germinate quickly and produce seedlings in one season. The seeds of the hybrid clematis may be very slow in germinating and may take up to three years.

DIVISION

Well established plants can be lifted and divided in the early spring. The division should be done with a sharp knife. The pieces of plant are then put straight into the ground prepared for clematis or, if they are small, planted in pots and later, when they are large enough, planted outside. This is a good method for producing new plants of the herbaceous clematis.

'NIBBLING'

'Nibbling' is different from root division. In nibbling the parent plant remains in the ground. Careful observation often reveals, especially in established plants, that the spread of the plant is so wide that it should be possible to nibble at it and take a piece away. You may even see an offshoot close to an established plant. Sometimes an established plant is so broad, it is possible to nibble away at two or three corners of it.

The golden rule of nibbling is that one must never risk damaging the parent plant. The roots of clematis go very deep. Therefore a sharp spade must be placed between the parent plant and the portion to be nibbled, and the spade driven deep into the ground separating the roots of the nibbled portion from that of the main plant. The spade is then withdrawn and driven in again at three places to complete a square around the portion to be nibbled. By pushing the spade in on the side which is most convenient, the nibbled part is then taken out of the ground. The nibbled portion, if large enough, can be grown in a prepared hole as usual, while a small portion can be potted into a large pot and then 'grown on' for another year.

GRAFTING

This is not a method now commonly employed in nurseries as inter-nodal cuttings have been found to be equally effective. Occasionally grafting is employed to produce plants more quickly; such plants can be strong specimens in the first season. Indeed the plant can be strong enough for it to be possible to take a number of cuttings from it that season.

HYBRIDIZING

Here one produces an entirely new plant by crossing one plant with another. For those who have the knowledge and the time, this is a most exciting aspect of clematis culture. It is a creative act to produce something which is unique and valuable. The principles are the same as for hybridizing in any genus and interested readers should consult specialist literature. In the appendix will be found reference to two articles on hybridizing clematis.

Short of the systematic-controlled hybridizing technique, the gardener can use two simple methods. Firstly, a sharp eye will notice chance clematis seedlings coming up in the garden. These can be potted up, grown on in pots and in two or three years may produce a bloom. It will be unique but usually disappointing. Rarely does this produce a new plant worth retaining by the gardener and, even more rarely, would it be accepted for sale by a nursery,

Secondly, without any attempt at deliberate hybridizing, and relying on chance fertilization, the seeds of any clematis can be taken and germinated in the way described above. The seedlings are potted up. Unique plants will be produced but again the great majority will be disappointing. Hope springs eternal!

The very attractive crimson blooms of C. texensis *'Gravetye Beauty' are shown against a background of seed heads and dried leaves. The species lends itself to such arrangements.*

APPENDIX

Clematis enthusiasts, or clematarians, can gain a great deal by talking to fellow enthusiasts about the plant. They will also benefit from visiting botanical gardens where clematis may be on display. Even more valuable are visits to specialist clematis nurseries where a wide range of plants can be seen from late spring to autumn, and where it is possible to decide more easily what appeals, and how a chosen plant will fit into your garden. Much information may also be gleaned about the best ways of growing the plant.

The surest way for the gardener to share knowledge with others is to join a horticultural society. There is such a society which caters for clematis, and this is the International Clematis Society. Clematis, after all, is an international plant; it is grown extensively throughout the temperate regions of the world.

The International Clematis Society started life in early 1984 by the initiative of Raymond J. Evison, then at Treasure's of Tenbury Nursery, Tenbury, UK. At once it began publishing a newsletter. Officers and a steering committee were set up. By the time of the International Conference in Sweden in June 1989, it was possible to agree a constitution and to establish a council and officers. Its journal, *Clematis International*, first appeared in 1988.

The aim of the International Clematis Society is to further the culture of clematis all over the world. It acts as a forum whereby knowledge can be shared by clematis enthusiasts all over the world. It furthers communication by newsletters and its journal. Regular meetings are held throughout the year in which there are lectures, slide shows and opportunity for open discussion. Plants can be bought at preferential rates at the meetings. The Society organizes a seed exchange. The Society's journal periodically publishes a list of the most popular clematis. From time to time, international conferences are held. The Society is affiliated to the Royal Horticultural Society based in London.

In Holland, an International Clematis Register of known clematis has been founded. It is expected that all new clematis will be registered there. There is already an extensive list of clematis in cultivation. This register was founded at the 21st International Horticultural Congress at Hamburg in 1982.

The International Clematis Society ultimately hopes to have a branch in many countries throughout the world. Its first branch was founded for its Great Britain and Ireland members in March 1990. It expects a rapid growth in membership as the plant has become so popular in recent years.

USEFUL ADDRESSES

International Clematis Society, 3 Route du Coudre, Rocquaine, St Pierre de Bois, Guernsey, Channel Islands, UK. Telephone: (0481) 45942.

Great Britain and Ireland Branch: 115 Belmont Road, Harrow, Middlesex, HA3 7PL, UK. Telephone: London (081)-427-5340.

Those wishing to join the Society, or make a Gift Subscription, can do so through the International Clematis Society, The Tropical Bird Gardens, Rode, Somerset, BA3 6QW, UK. Telephone: (0373) 830888.

The International Clematis Register, Department of Plant Taxonomy, Agricultural University, PO Box 8010, 6700 Ed, Wageningen, The Netherlands.

Two informative sources on hybridizing:

Chapter on 'Hybridizing' in *Clematis: The Queen of Climbers* by Jim Fisk, Cassell, 1989, London.

'An Amateur's Approach to Hybridization' by Vince and Sylvia Denny. Clematis International, 1989, International Clematis Society.

The viticellas are vigorous and hardy, easy to grow, and give a profusion of flowers in summer and autumn. C. viticella *'Purpurea Plena Elegans', seen here, has eye-catching violet-purple double flowers.*

INDEX

PUBLISHERS' ACKNOWLEDGEMENTS

The publishers are grateful to the following for granting permission to reproduce the following photographs: Photos Horticultural Picture Library (pp. 6, 8/9, 11, 12, 18, 22, 29, 32, 35, 61, 64, 69, 70, 73, 74, 77, 81, 82, 90, 93, 98, 104, 118/119 and 121); Harry Smith Horticultural Photographic Collection (pp. 24/25, 27, 41, 47, 53, 56, 58/59; Pat Brindley (p. 15); Betty Risdon, Tropical Bird Gardens (p. 54); J. Fisk (p. 117); T. Bennett (pp. 85 and 114); and K. Wolfenden (p.110).

All the line drawings were drawn by Nils Solberg.